# CONTENTS

*Introduction*     v

## BORDER-GAVASKAR TROPHY
### 9 Feb 2023 - 13 Mar 2023

| | |
|---|---|
| First Test | 3 |
| Second Test | 15 |
| Third Test | 27 |
| Fourth Test | 39 |

## INDIA V AUSTRALIA MEN'S ODI SERIES
### 17 Mar 2023 - 22 Mar 2023

| | |
|---|---|
| First ODI | 55 |
| Second ODI | 57 |
| Third ODI | 59 |

## ENGLAND V IRELAND

| | |
|---|---|
| Sole Test | 63 |

## WORLD TEST CHAMPIONSHIP FINAL

| | |
|---|---|
| Australia v India | 75 |

## THE MEN'S ASHES
### 9 Feb 2023 - 13 Mar 2023

| | |
|---|---|
| First Test | 95 |
| Second Test | 111 |

Third Test .................................................... 129

Fourth Test .................................................. 147

Fifth Test ..................................................... 161

## THE WOMEN'S ASHES
### 9 Feb 2023 - 13 Mar 2023

Test Match ................................................. 179

T20s .......................................................... 195

ODIs .......................................................... 201

## SOUTH AFRICA V AUSTRALIA MEN'S ODI SERIES
### 7 Sep 2023 - 27 Sep 2023

First ODI ..................................................... 211
Second ODI ................................................ 214
Third ODI ................................................... 217
Fourth ODI ................................................. 219
Fifth ODI .................................................... 222

*About the Author* ....................................... 227
*Also by Dan Liebke* .................................... 229

# DAN LIEBKE'S WASTED REVIEW OF CRICKET - 2023

DAN LIEBKE

# INTRODUCTION

For the past seven months, after just about every day's cricket I watched, I wrote a report card on the day's play for my supporters (over at newsletter.liebcricket.com and patreon.com/liebcricket, of course).

Those matches included pretty much every game the Australian men and women played (time zone pending, of course), most notably, the Border-Gavaskar Trophy and the men's and women's Ashes.

When you combine those various report cards together, you get this book - my wasted review of cricket in 2023 (more precisely, February 2023 to September 2023).

It's a detailed recap of my cricket watching over the past seven months, all done in what critics sneeringly refer to as my 'unique style'.

Enjoy reliving cricket in 2023.

## BORDER-GAVASKAR T

9 FEB 2023 - 13 MAR 202

# BORDER-GAVASKAR TROPHY

9 FEB 2023 - 13 MAR 2023

# FIRST TEST

## VIDARBHA CRICKET ASSOCIATION STADIUM, NAGPUR

# DAY ONE

REALITY TV SHOW PITCHES - GRADE: D

Heading into the first Test of the Border-Gavaskar Trophy, all talk was, tediously, about pitches. Is there anything more dull than pitch chat? Sure, of course there is. The world's a dull place, despite the best efforts of Prince Harry.

But if pitch chat isn't the *very* dullest thing in the world, it's in, like, the bottom one percentile. A tediously wearisome topic. If we must talk about pitches, then why not make it more interesting in the same way we've made it more interesting to hear people talking about renovating properties, finding dates, and getting celebrities out of here.

IDEA FOR REALITY TV SHOW: Different cricket pitches are prepared each week and judged by journalists from various cricket nations, each with their own unique biases. One by one, the pitches are eliminated until only one remains. That winner is... *Pitch Perfect*.

(A Test match is then played on it.)

DAN LIEBKE

## LUCIFER'S INFANTRY - GRADE: F

The other thing that people suddenly started talking about before the series even started was how stupid it was for Australia to have so many left-handers in their eleven.

As one of nature's opposite-monkeys myself, I found this offensive, but all the chatter got into Australia's head. Or, more precisely, Australia's Head, as Travis Head was startlingly replaced by the right-handed Peter Handscomb.

Having gone Full Henry the Eighth with the Head-axing, the tour selectors then also went Full Murphy's Law on fellow ink-smudger Ashton Agar, replacing him with bespectacled debutant Todd Murphy.

Great wordplay selection from Australia. But horrendous discrimination against the portfists. So much for Cummins' woke agenda.

## THINKING ABOUT JADEJA - GRADE: B+

Once the match started, the reverse-wretches who had escaped Cummins' cruel cackhander-culling were swiftly out, with both Usman Khawaja and David Warner skilfully negating the India spinners by being dismissed by the quicks in the opening overs.

> Dan Liebke @LiebCricket · 15h
> Test cricket in India is such a civilised time zone. Using the lunch break to grab an afternoon beer? Don't mind if I do. #INDvAUS #BorderGavaskarTrophy
> ◯ 2   ⟲   ♡ 43   ᴵ❙ᵢ 4,071   ⇧

With the run-scoring being rightfully left to the righties, Marnus Labuschagne and Steve Smith saw Australia safely to lunch and possible parity, but once they were out to Ravindra Jadeja shortly after the break, the vomit-mitts returned to the crease and India swiftly tore through them.

I'm annoyed that I so regularly forget how much fun Jadeja is. Genuinely mesmerising with ball, bat, and in the field. Probably a fascinating dinner guest as well, who always brings top tier wine and/or conversation. Jadeja feels like somebody I should think about every day and yet I know as soon as this series is over, he'll drift from my thoughts once again. It's my problem, not yours, Ravindra.

Matt Renshaw, promoted to bat at five, was out first ball to Jadeja. One can only assume that Head would have drilled his first ball straight back down the pitch and run out Smith at the non-striker's end? It was quite literally the only way he could have done worse.

Alex Carey came to the crease, completely out of the loop about the left-handed thing, and scored a breezy 36 at better than a run-a-ball, but that was the last glimmer of fun for Australia, as they were all out for 177 shortly after tea.

Still, about a hundred runs more than I expected. Good for them.

**Commentary Bits - Grade: B-**

India then cruelly flicked the pitch status to 'NOT doctored', as their openers serenely began the process of taking a first innings lead.

Fortunately, just as the final session started to feel predictable, Mark Waugh chimed in with some of his top tier nonsense. This time, to do with the ends of the VCA Stadium in Nagpur.

Inexplicably, Waugh suddenly demanded to know which was the north end and which was the south, even as shadows crept onto the ground from the afternoon sun. Great stuff from Junior. Full marks.

To be fair, compass directions aren't really the kind of thing a Julio would know. Definitely more a Nerd thing.

DAN LIEBKE

It wasn't the only bit the commentators were working on, however. At one point, several of the Indian commentators started having earnest discussions about what the home side might be comfortable chasing in the fourth innings.

LOL. Fourth innings. Right, guys.

> **Dan Liebke** @LiebCricket · 13h
> Australia win the first day by 100 runs. Congratulations to Pat Cummins and his team. #INDvAUS #BorderGavaskarTrophy
> 
> ◯ 1    ⇄ 9    ♡ 90    ıll 4,755    ⬆

# DAY TWO

### SCURRILOUS FOOTAGE - GRADE: F

Controversy overnight as footage went viral of Ravindra Jadeja applying a mysterious substance to his fingers. After the usual tiresome speculation played out, it was eventually revealed that the substance was a pain-relieving cream for his fingers, which were exhausted from dismissing so many Australian batters. Classic Jadeja - able to transfer even the scurrilous pressure of ball-tampering rumours back onto the opposition.

This wasn't the most disturbing vision to come out of India before the second day began, however. Because Matthew Hayden was spotted doing a pitch report in a hot pink cowboy hat.

Should Australia have come out this second morning with every fielder in a hot pink cowboy hat? If nothing else, it would have been an extraordinary show of unity that would have left India trembling.

Alas, it was just the usual baggy green. Probably some kind of Jane McGrath Day non-compete clause.

## MURPHYMANIA - GRADE: B+

Without the unifying force of rose-coloured stetsons, Australia turned instead to the man with the regular-coloured glasses, debutant Todd Murphy.

Murphy had taken the wicket of KL Rahul the evening before, caught and bowled, and on the second day began to steadily work his way through the rest of the India batting line-up.

Ravi Ashwin, Cheteshwar Pujara and Virat Kohli all fell to the bespectacled debutant, who seemingly had his corrected sights on taking all ten wickets in the innings.

> **Dan Liebke** @LiebCricket · Feb 9
> A Todd Murphy ten-fer? You're hearing it more and more. #INDvAUS #BorderGavaskarTrophy
> ♡ 6   ⟳ 4   ♡ 51   ᴵᴵᴵ 8,147   ⤒

Would Pat Cummins help him to the goal? Surely, if he simply removed Murphy's glasses every other over, he could bowl him at both ends, with the fool umpires none the wiser.

After the wicket of Kohli, it was fellow Test debutant Suryakumar Yadav's turn to face Murphy. It's always tough for a newcomer to the side to come up against a genuine cricketing superstar who has captured the world's imagination with his incredible feats.

Good luck, SKY.

## CARTWHEELING STUMPS - GRADE: A-

Sadly, Nathan Lyon ruined everything, as he so often does, the awful man. He dismissed SKY with one that turned between bat and pad and knocked the stump out of the ground, as Australia clawed their way back into the contest.

But almost as soon as they were back in, Rohit Sharma and Ravindra Jadeja Abe Simpsoned them straight back out, with a 61 run partnership.

Rohit made a century before Cummins took the new ball, gave him a warning by enticing an edge to the fumbling hands of Steve Smith before the very next ball sent his off stump cartwheeling out of the ground.

> **Dan Liebke** @LiebCricket · 14h
> Did one of the commentators just refer to Cummins as a medium pacer? Big fan of that kind of nonsense. #INDvAUS #BorderGavaskarTrophy
>
> ◯ 5   ⟲   ♡ 56   ᴵᴵᴵ 5,346   ⤴
>
> **Dan Liebke** @LiebCricket · 14h
> Sharpen up, Pat
>
> ◯   ⟲   ♡ 4   ᴵᴵᴵ 2,051   ⤴

I've said it before and I'll say it again. A cartwheeling stump should result in both batters being out.

Instead, Jadeja was unfairly permitted to continue on, pairing with Axar Patel to push India's lead well beyond one hundred.

Australia's only other success with the ball came via the People's Prince, Murphy, who trapped Srikar Bharat LBW to join the rest of the bowling line-up in having taken a five-fer on debut.

He had to win the wicket via DRS review, of course. Much like with Jadeja, the umpires' fingers were apparently extremely tender after such a busy time giving out Australians on the first day.

# DAY THREE

### SHAME - GRADE: D

The third morning began with Australia still needing three wickets. Todd Murphy, inevitably, was the man who got the first two, picking up the wicket of Jadeja early with one that went straight on. It's a delivery that I desperately hope he calls the 'oddball Todd ball'.

Mohammad Shami came in and started smacking sixes everywhere, apparently having misheard that bell-ringing 'shame, shame, shame' woman from *Games of Thrones*. This erroneous fictional support saw him reach 37 from 47 balls before Murphy got him, with Pat Cummins then finally tickling the edge of the stumps just enough to dislodge a bail and end both the innings of Axar Patel (84) and India (400).

India may have foolishly thought they were dominating the Test with their enormous first innings lead, but they weren't the side that unearthed Todd Murphy and must therefore feel as if they've missed a trick.

## PAT CUMMINS' PATIENCE - GRADE: B

Needing 223 to avoid an innings defeat, Australia started poorly, with Khawaja again out cheaply. Would Cummins promote himself to number three and hit a century? Really lead from the front? It's the kind of thing Allan Border would have done.

Instead, Cummins showed his tremendous patience, remained at his usual position of eight and was in, batting, within about half an hour, anyway.

Because Ravi Ashwin tore through the Australian top order, with wickets tumbling all over the place. Great stuff from Cummins' men, who comfortably ensured I'd be able to watch *Australian Survivor* tomorrow night. (Ironically, through their inability to survive.) Much appreciated.

It's fair to say Australia were unlucky, however. If this Test had been played in Sydney, it would've been rained out. Instead, it's in Nagpur. Fine margins such as these can decide a series.

At nine wickets down, Steve Smith would have been Jadeja's final victim of the Test had it not been for a no ball, which allowed him to continue on. A turning point in the Test? No, as it turned out.

Instead, Smith ended up being the not out batter, as Australia were eventually all out for 91. Should the rest of the Australian batting have simply batted like the second best batter the nation has ever produced? On reflection, you'd have to say 'yes'.

Still, on the plus side, 91 is way more than 36, so based on recent Border-Gavaskar Trophy precedent, Australia are 2.5 times more likely to win this series than India were a couple of years ago.

# SECOND TEST

ARUN JAITLEY STADIUM, DELHI

# DAY ONE

## DEALING WITH FIRST TEST AFTERMATH - GRADE: B

Following their big defeat in the first Test, Australia had a lot of factors to consider heading into the second.

Could they, for example, turn things around simply by having Steve Smith not giving thumbs up to bowlers who bowled a good ball? Perhaps. Certainly worth a try.

Should they play more spinners? Or go back to their fast bowlers? Rush Cameron Green back into the eleven to help balance the side? Select more right-handers? Or revert to left-handers? Almost too many options to weigh up.

In the end, the selectors decided on two changes. Travis Head returning in place of Matt Renshaw, and Scott Boland missing out, in favour of the left-arm spinner Matt Kuhnemann.

The selection met with predictable criticism. Matthew Hayden, in commentary, got properly stuck in, talking about how he vastly preferred the Australian blueprint of three fast bowlers and a spinner, but then halfway through explaining why this was his preference, he seemingly changed his mind completely. You may think that's a sign of how controversial the selection was, but it's pretty typical of Hayden's word salad brand of commentary.

Nevertheless, to avoid all the fuss, why didn't Australia simply go with the following XI?

1. Warner
2. Khawaja
3. Labuschagne
4. Smith
5. Head
6. Renshaw
7. Green
8. Handscomb
9. Carey (wk)
10. Agar
11. Starc
12. Cummins (c)
13. Murphy
14. Lyon
15. Kuhnemann
16. Hazlewood
17. Morris
18. Boland

Missed a trick there, for sure.

On the plus side, they won the toss, taking their streak to eight in a row in Test cricket. Coins are clearly as bewitched by Pat's handsomeness as the rest of us.

India, meanwhile, were celebrating Cheteshwar Pujara's hundredth Test. I sure hope at the end of this Test, Nathan Lyon celebrates the milestone by presenting Pujara with a commemorative shirt. Ideally, regifting the one India gave him a couple of years ago.

## SECRET SMOG - GRADE: F

Batting first, Australia reached fifty without loss, as David Warner and Usman Khawaja fought hard against the India attack, I imagine.

I had to imagine because the ground was covered in smog, making it extremely difficult to see anything that was going on. Was the smog to blame for Warner falling immediately after the half-century opening partnership was brought up? Probably not, unless it's been secretly smoggy every time he's toured India.

> Dan Liebke @LiebCricket · 19h
> Check the smog meters. #INDvAUS #BorderGavaskarTrophy

Marnus Labuschagne replaced Warner at the crease, had some fun on his way to 18, before he was trapped in front by Ravi Ashwin. That brought Smith to the middle, giving thumbs up to everybody he saw, like some demented Fonz. Getting into the spirit of things, Smith also rode to the middle on a motorcycle, wearing a leather jacket. He then immediately jumped a shark, caught behind from Ashwin's second ball.

> Dan Liebke @LiebCricket · 18h
> Australia still with all their reviews. Well on top here. #INDvAUS #BorderGavaskarTrophy

Australia therefore went to lunch on 3/94. Advantage India? Advantage Australia? No, advantage cricket fans, who had the New Zealand-England Test (see my *Wasted Review of Cricket - 2022/23*) resuming precisely as the India-Australia one went to a break.

This is how it's done, ICC.

## OPENING THE BOWLING - GRADE: D

After lunch, Australia stammered and stumbled their way to 263 all out. Khawaja was the backbone of the early part of the innings, scoring a fun-filled 81, before he was Kaught Ludicrously by KL Rahul.

The back portion of the innings then saw Peter Handscomb add 95 runs with the last four wickets, courtesy primarily of Pat Cummins, who tonked a few sixes into the crowd, showing the Nighthawk, batting simultaneously over in Mount Maunganui, exactly how it was done.

The first change of innings is the best part of a Test in India. The point where everybody can briefly believe 263 is a decent score before India spend two days amassing 600.

Cummins' work wasn't done, however. After Australia were all out, India had nine overs to face. With Cummins the sole fast bowler in the team, who would open the bowling alongside him? Marnus Labuschagne bowling seam-up? Pat Cummins wearing Todd Murphy's spectacles? Maybe the Nighthawk's close personal friend Stuart Broad?

No, it turned out to be Matt Kuhnemann, which raised the obvious question, when was the last time an Australian slow bowler opened the bowling on Test debut?

(Answer: Glenn McGrath)

# DAY TWO

### CONCUSSED HAIRLINE FRACTURES OF THE ELBOW - GRADE: C-

On the second morning, Pat Cummins took on board my day one suggestion that Australia take the game to India via the simple tactic of playing more than eleven cricketers in the Test.

For follow-up testing after David Warner's battered innings the day before revealed that the Australian opener now had a concussed hairline fracture of the elbow and was therefore out of the Test.

An opportunity for Australia? Would Mitchell Starc be deemed a like-for-like replacement? Common sense said: yes. Instead, Matt Renshaw - a man who simply refuses to play Test cricket normally - was summoned into the match.

Not that this appeased Sunil Gavaskar in commentary, who finds concussion substitutes a modern-day disgrace.

With Allan Border furious at Steve Smith for thumbs-upping the India bowlers and Gavaskar claiming that concussion substitutes are a reward for not being able to play the short ball, the Border-Gavaskar Trophy is surely now the most boomer prize in world cricket.

## BURNING REVIEWS - GRADE: A

Once play started, Australia had another next-level tactic up their sleeve, burning all three of their reviews in the opening half hour.

At first, fans back home were thinking 'What is Cummins doing? Why don't Australia simply review the ones that are out and not review the ones that aren't out?'

Mark Waugh, in commentary, echoed the thoughts of those back-home fans, although he got things rather muddled up, as you'd expect. His musings that Australia would be without reviews for the next 65 overs both a) suggested he believed reviews are still renewed after 80 overs, and also b) got the maths wrong anyway. Classic stuff from Junior.

In fact, it turned out that by burning all their reviews early, Australia received the subconscious benefit of tight umpire's calls. Next level play from Cummins and his men.

> Dan Liebke @LiebCricket · 17h
> Reviews are for the weak of spirit, anyway. Correct to burn them.
> #INDvAUS #BorderGavaskarTrophy
> ○       ↻ 2       ♡ 19       ıl 2,144       ⬆

## GOAT ATTACKS - GRADE: B-

Nathan Lyon didn't need reviews anyway. Oh, sure, he missed out on a wicket because Cummins refused to use one on a rejected LBW shout against Cheteshwar Pujara that was going on to hit the stumps, but that was all part of the master plan.

After all, what could be more humiliating for Pujara than being out for a pair in the first innings of his hundredth Test? Because that's what happened a few balls later when Lyon trapped him yet again, still without a run on the board and with the umpire this time getting the ole finger out.

Lyon took the first four wickets to fall, and five in total, accounting for not just Pujara, but also Rohit Sharma, KL Rahul, Shreyas Iyer and Srikar Bharat as India crumbled to 7/139.

> Dan Liebke @LiebCricket · 15h
> Lyon ruins Murphy's ten-fer in the first Test. Murphy returning the favour here. #INDvAUS #BorderGavaskarTrophy

"Excuse me, Delhi police? I'd like to report a goat attack."

### TAKING OUTLANDISH CATCHES - GRADE: B

But just when Australia thought they might take a lead of more than a hundred into the second innings, Axar Patel and Ravi Ashwin put on a magnificent 114 run partnership to drag the match back India's way.

The pair got within ten runs of Australia's total before Australia found the key to dismissing them. That key? Taking outlandish catches.

First, Renshaw snaffled one off a new ball loosener from Cummins on Ashwin's pads. Then Cummins chipped in with a terrified grab of a powerfully hit Axar straight swat.

Combined with Peter Handscomb's earlier improbable grab at short leg, it proved the age-old cricketing axiom: No reviews = clear minds = safe hands.

In my opinion, Australian fielders should keep taking freak catches if they want to win. Good game plan. Worth persevering with.

# DAY THREE

### FULFILLING BRIEFS - GRADE: C

Australia's one run first innings lead gave them leeway to bat like kings in their second innings and they proceeded to do so on the third day, sweeping wildly from an overnight score of 1/61 to 113 all out.

Everybody was guilty of underperforming with the bat. Well, except perhaps for Matt Renshaw, who perfectly fulfilled the brief of batting like a concussed David Warner. He made two before being trapped LBW by Ashwin, bringing to an end the R Ashwin v Renshaw tussle, one of the great near-anagram cricket battles.

Ashwin (3/59) and Ravindra Jadeja (7/42) took all ten wickets to fall, bewildering the Australian batters on a pitch with faltering bounce. And yet, I have exclusive learned that this pair - India's so-called 'spin twins' - are not only not twins, but aren't even siblings! Come on, India. Enough shenanigans.

The collapse got all the talking heads infuriated, and all the infuriated heads talking:

"Why don't the Australians simply bat like Rohit Sharma, a batter with vastly more experience in these conditions than them who isn't facing Ashwin and Jadeja?" they steamed. "Can't believe they haven't thought of trying this."

## THE BLAME TRAIN - GRADE: B+

All those angry people risked feeling awfully silly in their outrage if Australia's spin sextuplets (Nathan Lyon, Todd Murphy, Matthew Kuhnemann, Travis Head, Marnus Labuschagne and Steve Smith) rolled India for 70.

Because, as bad as Australia's collapse to 113 all out might have seemed, their first innings lead meant India needed *115* to win, rather than 114. Advantage Australia.

Or, as it turned out, not, as India completed a six wicket victory to take an unbeatable 2-0 lead in the Border-Gavaskar Trophy and really get the blame train rolling.

I say, if we're going to blame anyone for this defeat, we should blame that guy who turned 50 and invited Glenn Maxwell to his party.

# THIRD TEST

HOLKAR CRICKET STADIUM, INDORE

# DAY ONE

## INDORE CRICKET WORDPLAY - GRADE: D

The third Test was played at Indore, which raised the prospect of an endless supply of Indore/indoor cricket wordplay, something to take Australians' minds off their inevitable thrashing. A lovely touch from the BCCI.

Alas, however, the Indore Test was not scheduled to be played with indoor cricket rules. A ghastly missed opportunity for everybody involved. I mean, what are we even doing, people?

Nevertheless, perhaps understandable when you consider the turning nature of the pitch and remember that lost wickets in indoor cricket result in a loss of runs. Were the Indore cricket scoreboards set up for negative totals in every innings? If not, fair enough to apply normal Test match playing conditions.

The first session saw wickets tumble to spin, as everybody expected. What was unexpected, however, was that they were Indian wickets, with Steve Smith cleverly losing the toss and allowing India to bat first.

Good thinking from Smith to ensure Australia wouldn't be bowled out in the first session. (Although, at one point, with India 5/45 after 11.2 overs, sensible followers of the game weren't willing to rule anything out.)

## MORAL VICTORIES - GRADE: B+

Of course, the reason that Smith was captaining was because Pat Cummins had returned home. Cummins' absence, and a healed finger, also allowed Mitchell Starc to return to the team.

Starc got immediately carried away - apparently not realising that it was a spinner's pitch - and took the wicket of Rohit Sharma first ball caught behind before also trapping him LBW later in that over.

Great bowling from Starc, who would therefore have been disappointed to see Rohit batting on well into the second over and beyond. The reason for this was that the umpires couldn't be bothered giving the Indian captain out, and Smith couldn't be bothered reviewing either of the shouts.

> Dan Liebke @LiebCricket · 17h
> Anyway, good to see the umpires are keeping their fingers well rested.
> #INDvAUS #BorderGavaskarTrophy

Can't burn reviews if you never use them. That's the Smith philosophy. Good thinking.

Rarely have I seen a Test in which the moral victor was established so quickly. After just one over and Smith's judicious use of non-reviews, Rohit and the rest of the India team were left playing for the sad, secondary prize of an actual victory. Advantage Australia.

As the dismissals that weren't given or reviewed in Starc's first over were replayed on the big screen, however, it did raise one important question.

How many wickets wouldn't Starc take in his second over?

## UNTRUSTWORTHY PARTNERSHIPS - GRADE: D

With the moral victory sewn up, Australia turned their sights to actual victory, foolishly tearing through India's batting line up with sharp-turning deliveries that also occasionally kept low.

Silly stuff from Australia, who must surely have known they were doomed if they ever had to bat on the pitch. Why not instead let India bat for five days? Refuse to accept declarations. Take a draw.

> **Dan Liebke** @LiebCricket · 16h
> Always give the quick an over before lunch. #INDvAUS #BorderGavaskarTrophy
> 〇 1  ⟲ 1  ♡ 9  ᴨ 1,799  ⇪

Bowling India all out could only lead to trouble. And yet, shortly after lunch, Australia completed their mauling of the home side, dismissing them for 109.

> **Dan Liebke** @LiebCricket · 15h
> The commentators, whether Australian or Indian, all agree: the Australian bowlers should be trying to get these two out. #INDvAUS #BorderGavaskarTrophy
> 〇 2  ⟲ 3  ♡ 13  ᴨ 2,838  ⇪

In reply, Travis Head fell early and Marnus Labuschagne did that thing he does where he's the luckiest man in the universe, being recalled after dragging a Jadeja delivery onto his stumps because the bowler overstepped.

Labuschagne and Usman Khawaja then put together a 96 run partnership, taking them to the brink of first innings parity with India.

Pretty suspicious stuff if you ask me. A partnership that couldn't be trusted one bit. It was unclear exactly what was going on or who was responsible, but I did. not. trust. it.

I mean, were we supposed to take it at face value? That these two could just score runs at will when India as a collective barely broke a hundred? No. It didn't add up. I don't know what the scam was supposed to be, but I refuse to fall for it.

Anyway, good to see that these Australian batters have worked so hard in the last ten days on the moral failings that cost them their wickets in the first two Tests.

## THE MARNUS OF INDIA REVIEWS - GRADE: B-

India, however, didn't let up. Particularly Ravindra Jadeja - the Marnus of India reviews - who enthusiastically convinced Rohit to send LBW appeals upstairs three times, only to have them knocked back on each occasion.

As the old saying goes, fool me once, shame on Jadeja. Fool me twice, shame on Rohit. Fool me three times, shame on everybody involved in the entire DRS process. But, y'know, mostly Jadeja.

On the plus side for Jadeja, however, he did end the day with more wickets than burnt reviews, finishing with all four of the Australian wickets to fall.

Sure, Jadeja also cost Ravi Ashwin a wicket with his overly ambitious pleas for reviews leaving Rohit too battle-scarred to send an Ashwin shout upstairs. But as far as I can tell, that still leaves him even.

Tune in for the second day to follow this enthralling tussle between the number of reviews and wickets Jadeja burns and the number he takes. Could be a thriller.

# DAY TWO

### A MYSTERIOUS LACK OF AGGRESSION - GRADE: C

Australia began the second day trying desperately to stretch out their lead. Cameron Green and Peter Handscomb slowly but surely inched their way to a forty run partnership, as the commentators urged them to bat with greater intent and accelerate the scoring.

Why weren't these Australian batters scoring faster by playing the more aggressive shots they were pilloried for playing in the previous Test? Sadly, we may never know.

Eventually, however, Handscomb was dismissed by Ravi Ashwin, caught in close, and the introduction of India's fastest spinner through the air, Umesh Yadav, finished off Green and the tail as Australia lost 6/11 to be all out for 197, a lead of 88 on the first innings.

Should wickets taken by fast bowlers on this spinner's pitch be overturned by the third umpire? Common sense says: yes.

Presumably, this is why Australia didn't review the wickets that Starc took but weren't given. They knew what kind of pitch it was and were determined to play by those guidelines. Typically strong adherence to the spirit of the game by Steve Smith.

## JOEL WILSON'S VENDETTA - GRADE: B+

Batting a second time, India unluckily lost Shubman Gill, out trying to wipe out the first innings deficit in one shot.

He was the first wicket to fall to Nathan Lyon, but by no means the last, as Lyon toiled hard against the opposition to take the spectacular figures of 8/64 from 23.3 overs.

By 'opposition', I mostly mean, of course, umpire Joel Wilson, who continued his ongoing stance of never, ever giving Nathan Lyon an LBW. It was true in 2019 in Headingley and it was still true in this Test. And fair enough, too. Senseless vendettas are the lifeblood of Test cricket.

(And don't you dare try to come at me with stats that prove otherwise. Facts are meaningless. Vibes are everything.)

## FARMYARD CRUELTY - GRADE: D

As India snuck their way into the lead via an outstanding innings from Cheteshwar Pujara, Australia strained desperately to limit their fourth innings run chase.

> **Dan Liebke** @LiebCricket · 14h
> "They've been quite tidy, the Australian spinners."
>
> (cut to Kuhnemann covered in filth from head to toe) #INDvAUS #BorderGavaskarTrophy
>
> ○   ⟲   ♡ 15   ᴉ₁ᴉ 1,792   ⤴

Again, they reverted to their tiresome stealth caught behind reviews via stumping appeals. A bit of fun once or twice, guys, yes, but now, dull and shameless. I say, give the batters a free hit every time a stumping appeal is turned down. That'll put an end to it.

As Lyon stretched his calf, in obvious pain (a GOAT stretching a calf? Somebody stop this farmyard cruelty!), India's lead threatened to similarly stretch beyond Australia's reach.

That's when Steve Smith took a breathtaking leg slip catch, diving to his right to snare an edge from Pujara low to the ground.

Lots of talk before the match that the responsibility of the captaincy would bring out Smith's best batting form. It felt notable, then, that he only scored 26, showing instead his support for Pat Cummins' leadership. But this catch, when he'd been a hopeless duffer in the cordon in the first two Tests, suggests that perhaps Smith is making a play for longer term leadership.

Either way, Smith was definitely ecstatic with the grab, which ensured Australia would only have to chase 76 on the third and final day.

Partly because the catch got rid of Pujara. Partly because it showed he was still a reliable force in the slips. But mostly, I think, because Marnus Labuschagne had dropped Pujara earlier from a much less spectacular attempt.

That's how it's done, Marnus.

# DAY THREE

### THE VERY HIGHEST OF NUMBERS - GRADE: D

Australia's hard work on the first two days ensured they would only have to chase 76 on the third and final day.

Still, most mathematicians agree that 76 is among the very highest of numbers and, going into the day's play, it felt both insane and perfectly justified that the result of this Test was not yet completely certain.

This feeling intensified when Usman Khawaja was out second ball of the day. Travis Head and Marnus Labuschagne, however, came together to defend furiously against India's spinslaught.

Labuschagne even trialled a new tactic of refusing to face up to Ravi Ashwin as he came in to bowl. Can't take my wicket if you don't deliver the ball seemed to be Marnus's reasoning. Sound logic, too (as long as Head remained in his crease at the non-striker's end).

Eventually, however, the umpires had a word with Labuschagne and explained to him the basic idea of cricket as a contest between bat and ball, convincing him to not pull away every time Ashwin came in to bowl.

A disappointed Labuschagne reluctantly got on board with the idea, only for Ashwin to then pull out of his run up.

Excellent stuff. A great little period of nobody playing any cricket. Only cricket can offer such a lack of cricket.

MONKEY'S PAW CRICKET BALLS - GRADE: B-

Unable to get through Labuschagne and Head's defences, India asked the umpires if they could have a new ball that might offer more assistance in that area.

Certainly, came the reply.

But it was a monkey's paw of a ball. Yes, Australia's batters could no longer defend against the India bowling. But that was only because they suddenly exploded into attack against it.

Head started blasting boundaries everywhere. Labuschagne followed suit, and before anybody knew what had happened, Australia found themselves winning the Test by nine wickets.

> **Dan Liebke** @LiebCricket · 17h
> Proper cricket ball, this one. Great sportsmanship from India to change it.
> #INDvAUS #BorderGavaskarTrophy
> ◯ 3   ⟲ 1   ♡ 49   ᴨ 3,726   ⇪

In doing so, Australia booked themselves a place in the World Test Championship final. Kind of an elaborate process to get there, you might think, but it's still infinitely simpler than using the Ticketek website.

# FOURTH TEST

NARENDRA MODI STADIUM, AHMEDABAD

# DAY ONE

### NARENDRA MODI STADIUM - GRADE: D-

Before this Test started at the Narendra Modi Stadium, a lucky Prime Minister who happened to share the same name as the ground was given the opportunity for a free ride around the playing arena in the back of a car that had giant cardboard cricket bats protruding from the back of it for some reason.

Prime Minister Stadium and his invited guest, Australian Prime Minister, Anthony McG, were paraded around in front of adoring crowds who waved enthusiastically at the twin leaders. Sadly, however, the excellent political grandstanding was eventually interrupted by some actual Test cricket. Booo!

Luckily, Mohammad Shami livened things up in the first over by spraying the ball all over the place, out of reach of batter and keeper alike. Would Australia finish the first day on 0/250 (Usman Khawaja 0*, Travis Head 0*)? It seemed possible.

Sadly, Khawaja ruined this dream, edging the sixth ball of the innings between the slips for four.

Still, dreams may come and go, but they never stop coming, as my Grandad used to say. (He was very old.) With further byes and no balls in the early overs, the prospect arose instead of a new dream. A dream that the oldest Test record - Bannerman's record of highest proportion of runs in a completed innings - might finally be broken by extras.

But no. That one didn't work either. Dreams are for suckers and ne'er-do-wells, as my Grandad also used to say. Kill your dreams and kill them dead.

## SECRET STUMP SESSIONS - GRADE: B+

Speaking of dreams, though, it was the middle session that provided the best opportunity for a wee nap, as Khawaja and Steve Smith batted serenely under no threat from any of the India bowlers. (Khawaja would eventually go on to make a century. Doin' it for Albo.)

Any session you can safely snooze through is a great session. Fine stuff from both sides. Proper Test cricket. It stands in stark contrast to those dreadful Bazball Tests, where even a twenty-minute doze sees you running the risk of waking up in a transformed hellscape where everything you've previously known is gone forever.

Still, if you did want to make an innings more frantic, why not have a secret stump session, in which the fielding team is allowed to give the off stump to a secret fielder to hide in the back of their shirt. During that time, the batter is only permitted to leave the ball if they can tell the umpire or opposition captain who has the missing stump. Batters are always banging on about knowing where their off stump is. Let them prove it.

## COMMENTARY NONSENSE - GRADE: A

With the cricket wonderfully sedate, the commentators tried hard to capture our attention. Matthew Hayden attempted a Ferrari analogy that was highly detailed but went nowhere (maybe because of a busted carburettor? I don't know much about cars). He also had detailed theories about what the batters should be doing differently that he didn't hesitate to thrust violently at us, the innocent viewer.

I'm quite certain Hayden knows infinitely more than I do about batting in a Test match and yet every word he utters somehow makes me doubt that self-evident truth. A gift.

As good as Hayden was, however, Sunil Gavaskar trumped him effortlessly, at one point delving deep into Mark Waugh's bag of tricks and pulling an 'I haven't seen much of him' on Steve Smith. Wonderful stuff from Gavaskar. Wish he'd expanded it further.

"This Kohli chap. What's his go?"

"That Stokes fellow? Is he a bowler or a batter? A bit of both? Huh. Good for him."

And so on and so forth.

# DAY TWO

## GIANT PUPPIES - GRADE: A-

Usman Khawaja and Cameron Green continued their partnership into the second day of the Test. Could Green - the biggest puppy in world cricket - finally get his first century for Australia?

He could, and he should, and he would, eventually cutting Ravi Jadeja for four to bring up the ton. Good puppy. Good giant puppy.

> **Dan Liebke** @LiebCricket · 17h
> GIVE THE GIANT PUPPY A TON! #INDvAUS #BorderGavaskarTrophy
> ♡ 1   ⟲ 1   ♡ 46   ᴵᴵᴵ 6,222   ↑

> **Dan Liebke** @LiebCricket · 17h
> He's been a good boy. He deserves it. #INDvAUS #BorderGavaskarTrophy
> ♡ 1   ⟲    ♡ 13   ᴵᴵᴵ 1,550   ↑

Probably the only disappointment was that he didn't bring up the milestone while wearing a baggy green. Or, for that matter, wearing clothes a couple of sizes too big for him, so that he *was* a baggy Green. Or, ideally, both. Ah well, maybe next Test century.

(And, yes, we know it's hard to find clothes a couple of sizes too big for Cameron Green, but that doesn't mean we shouldn't try!)

Green and Khawaja's partnership eventually reached 208 before Green was out.

I wholeheartedly disapprove of the Australian cricket team playing competently in India. It is against the natural order of things and a stain on the game. Would another year's suspension for those involved sort the situation out?

It couldn't hurt, surely.

## TACTICAL DEFICIENCIES - GRADE: C

Khawaja also fell, first ball after tea, veering away from his plan of middling every delivery that came his way and instead missing one from Axar Patel that struck him in front.

A silly change in tactics from Khawaja, one that gave India access to the tail and the inevitable rapid conclusion to the innings.

Instead, Nathan Lyon and Todd Murphy added a further seventy runs to the total, enough to inexplicably have commentators talking about declarations.

No, no, no, no! Seeing your tailenders who've tallied about a dozen runs between them throughout the series smack the bowlers all around the place should make you *less* likely to want to get out there and bowl. Not more likely. What is wrong with people? I've said it before and I'll say it again. Never declare. Bat forever if you can.

The other benefit to Lyon and Murphy's partnership was that it helped Australia reach 480 all out, and, more importantly, tire India after two long days in the field under the sweltering sun. That's good Test cricket.

Silly old England would have made 480 runs on day one, leaving India barely exhausted. They probably would have declared as well. A tactically deficient team, but trying their best. That's all we can ask of them.

## WASTING EVERYBODY'S TIME - GRADE: F

As if to prove my point, the India openers, Rohit Sharma and Shubman Gill, faced ten overs and effortlessly knocked 36 runs off the deficit for the loss of no wicket.

Why, I've seen entire India teams dismissed for 36 runs, and here the openers were, amassing that total without breaking a sweat.

As if to rub in how easy it was for them, Shubman Gill wasted everybody's time in the final over of the day by crashing a six into an area of the stadium where it was almost impossible to retrieve the ball. A lot of nonsense, then, with everybody ready to call it a day, but having to stick around while a replacement ball was summoned even as an intrepid crowd member heroically found their way to the lost, original ball.

Should Australia have been allowed to bowl with both balls? Twice the chance for wickets, yes, but also twice the chance for the openers to smash them to the boundary. Let's trial it in The Hundred first before we make it a Test cricket option.

Less controversially, I propose that if a batter hits a six that delays the game, they should be eligible to be timed out. Keep a cumulative tally of the time they waste and, once they pass the permitted time, get rid of them. Good riddance to six-hitting rubbish, I say.

# DAY THREE

## LYRICAL ENTHUSIASM - GRADE: B

On a pitch that offered little assistance to the bowlers, India continued their steady march to matching (and then inevitably surpassing) Australia's first innings total, with Shubman Gill, in particular, cruising along to an untroubled century.

> **Dan Liebke** @LiebCricket · 17h
> India have avoided the follow-on. (I mean, not technically, but it's only a matter of time.) #INDvAUS #BorderGavaskarTrophy
> ◯ 2   ⟲ 2   ♡ 16   ᵢₗᵢ 5,156   ⬆

As India batted, we slowly gleaned one of the benefits of the pitches from earlier in the series, a virtue we may not have appreciated at the time. Namely, that we only ever had to listen to Matthew Hayden for three days.

As annoying as Hayden was, however, the dominance of bat over ball for the first time in the series also finally gave the India commentators an opportunity to indulge in their favourite pastime of gushing with lyrical enthusiasm over the strokeplay of the batters. It was an opportunity they did not hesitate to take, which added a fresh flavour to the day's play.

Example piece of commentary:

> (Batter hits a boundary)
>
> Indian commentator: This sublime genius, his unparalleled skill giving us a glimpse into the heavenly realms, the crack of the bat a transcendent song welcoming us into a higher state of bliss, the timing of his shot a hint of the clockwork nature of the cosmos, ticking along with the orderly beauty of a wisdom greater than we dare contemplate
>
> Australian commentator: Yes, but also shit bowling.

## MUSCLE HICCUPS - GRADE: D

With no other way to dismiss the India batters, Australia pulled into their Cricket Australia-endorsed bag of tricks, and pulled out the rarely used tactic of letting their opponents bat so long they get cramp.

Ruthless stuff from the Australians, but also effective stuff as Gill eventually succumbed for 128 after suffering from the ol' muscle hiccups.

As the day ended with India on 3/289, Australia could look back on their work with pride, safe in the knowledge that, at this rate, they would bowl India out early on day six.

# DAY FOUR

VIRAT KOHLI - GRADE: A-

**M**ost of the fourth day was the same as the third with Virat Kohli reprising the Shubman Gill role and scoring a century.

The ton sent the fans at the ground (including everybody in the commentary box) into a rapturous frenzy, as the great man broke his Test century drought in emphatic style, eventually reaching 186 before he was last man out, caught trying to thrash some final runs with only the tail for company.

I don't want to get carried away, but I think Virat Kohli's centuries make his fans almost as happy as Glenn Maxwell's centuries make his.

The Kohli century was all part of a steady acceleration by the India batters, as first Ravindra Jadeja, and then Srikar Bharat combined with Kohli to run down, then surpass Australia's total.

The entire day's play was so pre-ordained that at one point I watched a full episode of *Australian Survivor* and returned to find the same partnership still going. Another area in which Kohli dominates the greats of the past.

> Dan Liebke @LiebCricket · 15h
> I can't even keep track of what's real and what's replay at the moment. Sirens. Sixes. Sad Cameron Green. It's all a blur. #INDvAUS #BorderGavaskarTrophy
>
> ○   ↻   ♡ 32   ıl 2,936   ⬆

## MULTI-DIMENSIONAL CRICKET - GRADE: B

India finished their first innings 91 runs ahead of Australia with just fifteen minutes or so remaining in the day.

The looming World Test Championship Final added an extra fascinating element to the final stages of not just this Test but also the one taking place over in New Zealand between the home side and Sri Lanka.

For India to definitively join Australia in the WTC Final, they need to either win this Test or have Sri Lanka *not* win their Test.

However, Sri Lanka are on target to defeat New Zealand, putting pressure back on India to press for victory here. This is multi-dimensional cricket, across different hemispheres and only partially shared time zones. A fascinating contest that requires serious concentration and thought.

Or, if you're Australia and have already qualified for the final, you can have some fun and open your batting with Matt Kuhnemann as nightwatchman. A nightwatchkuhnemann!

Why not? Kuhnemann and Travis Head survived six overs in the final session to finish on 0/3. At this rate of scoring, Australia will be only 40 runs behind when stumps are called on the final day.

# DAY FIVE

## EXTENDING TESTS - GRADE: D

There wasn't much excitement left in the Test entering the final day. (Well, not in the India-Australia Test. We'll get to other sources of excitement shortly.)

Most of the intrigue for the day settled on new Australian opener Matthew Kuhnemann.

Can a man named Kuhnemann bat through the session?

Can a man named Kuhnemann score his first Test century?

Can a man named Kuhnemann carry his bat?

Perhaps, but not in this Test, robbed of an opportunity by an LBW that Travis Head refused to let him review.

Instead, Head and Marnus Labuschagne and later Steve Smith batted tediously through the day, still unruffled by any of the bowling, safely seeing Australia to the safety of a draw.

Should the six days lost earlier in the series have been added onto the end of this Test? It'd still have been a draw, of course, but at least we'd have got to see, I dunno, Mitchell Starc and Todd Murphy put on 200 together.

## NEW ZEALAND - GRADE: B+

The reason that neither side particularly cared about striving for anything other than a draw in the Test was not just because a result was impossible on such a benign pitch (although, sure, that was part of it).

It was also because over in Christchurch, New Zealand had snuck home against Sri Lanka in a final ball, two wicket thriller (just a week or so after a gripping one run win after following on against England), ensuring India joined Australia in the World Test Championship final.

An absolute thriller that came down to Kane Williamson and Neil Wagner haring a bye from the last ball of the Test to secure the win, while Sri Lanka attempted at least two run outs to salvage their own draw.

In a way, I'm disappointed that Sri Lanka didn't run out Williamson off that final ball to secure a draw. I'd have loved to have both the India-Australia Test and the New Zealand-Sri Lanka one finish with technically the same result.

But it didn't and so I therefore propose that all future Test cricket takes place in New Zealand.

# INDIA V AUSTRALIA MEN'S ODI SERIES

17 MAR 2023 - 22 MAR 2023

# FIRST ODI

## WANKHEDE STADIUM, MUMBAI

### THE ENGINE OF MATHEMATICS - GRADE: D

With David Warner not having recovered from his elbow injury, Mitchell Marsh was promoted to open alongside Travis Head.

Marsh made the most of his time at the top, crashing a century within the first ten overs. Or so it seemed, as he hammered boundary after thumping boundary. Yet, in defiance of our understanding of basic arithmetic, it still took him 51 balls to raise his half-century, with 46 of those runs coming from fours and sixes.

Luckily, Marnus Labuschagne got tinkering with the engine of mathematics and sorted out Marsh's problem, which allowed him to accelerate properly to 81 (65) before finally being dismissed by Ravi Jadeja.

Great work from Marsh, who, with Shaun's recent retirement is surely aware that the final outcome of the great Mitches v Marshes battle that has defined Australian cricket for the last decade is now squarely in his hands. Just as the prophecy foretold.

For while he is undeniably a Mitch, he is now also the last of the Marshes (at least until the next generation comes along). A big decade looming for him.

### ALL-ROUNDERS - GRADE: D-

Marsh's wicket saw Australia collapse from 2/129 to 188 all out. They had selected a side full of all-rounders, batting all the way to nine. Not enough, clearly, and I look forward to the next ODI in which they select a lineup that bats all the way to at least fifteen or twenty.

Nevertheless, very kind of the Australians to give an opportunity for those of us back home to watch the entire match rather than just the first innings.

A nice thought, for sure, but the half-hour innings break in which Foxtel gave us an Australia victory over India in a 1992 World Series Cup match, followed by highlights of the women cruising to their trillionth World Cup win in the recent T20 final was enough to send most Australians to bed. Peter Taylor and Ashleigh Gardner wielding their decades-separated magic? Sweet dreams.

❄

### MORPHEUS OFF THE SHORT RUN

Here's what I missed in the second innings, in limerick form:

> *Defending a small total, here comes Mitch Starc*
> *Tearing through the top order, some hope, just a spark,*
> *But KL Rahul,*
> *Who's nobody's fool,*
> *Guided India safely past the 188 mark*

# SECOND ODI

## DR. Y.S. RAJASEKHARA REDDY ACA-VDCA CRICKET STADIUM, VISAKHAPATNAM

### PREPARING FOR BED - GRADE: F

Well, uh, that was quick. I saw a few early wickets from Mitchell Starc, turned over to watch *Australian Survivor*, returned in ad breaks to see still more wickets fall, then as I was brushing my teeth and removing my contact lenses (not simultaneously), Travis Head and Mitchell Marsh finished the entire thing off.

> **Dan Liebke** @LiebCricket · 12h
> I'll watch Starc's hat trick attempt but then it's #SurvivorAU time. #INDvAUS
> ♡ 1   ⟳   ♡ 7   ⬚ 3,955   ⬆

> **Dan Liebke** @LiebCricket · 12h
> Literally turned back in the ad break, said 'come on, Starc, take another wicket'. And he did. Are… are all cricketers my puppets? #INDvAUS
> ♡ 4   ⟳   ♡ 8   ⬚ 2,843   ⬆

> **Dan Liebke** @LiebCricket · 11h
> Back in time to see Ellis get Jadeja. Proper cricket, this. #INDvAUS
> ♡   ⟳   ♡ 4   ⬚ 1,477   ⬆

Still, lovely to see that Dave Warner got a free flight to India to watch the end of his career score 121 in 11 overs.

DAN LIEBKE

## MORPHEUS OFF THE SHORT RUN

Here's the match in limerick form:

> *Mitchell Starc killed India's innings stone dead,*
> *The grave was then danced on by Mitch Marsh and*
>     *Trav Head*
> *A blitz of biffing and bashing*
> *Concluded the thrashing,*
> *Should have probably just played a T20 instead.*

# THIRD ODI

## MA CHIDAMBARAM STADIUM, CHENNAI

### DAVID WARNER BATTING DOWN THE ORDER - GRADE: D

Again, I didn't get to see much of the match. A bit of Australia's innings, with David Warner selected as a specialist bowler, scheduled to bat at nine (I assume), before I headed to bed during a drinks break.

❋

### MORPHEUS OFF THE SHORT RUN

Here's the match in limerick form:

> *5/138, an Australia innings in flux,*
> *Became a 270 target - good, not deluxe*
> *But Agar and Adam Zampa*
> *Made Smith a happy camper*
> *Including a hat trick of SKY golden ducks*

# ENGLAND V IRELAND

# SOLE TEST

## LORD'S, LONDON

# DAY ONE

## SKIVVIED ALFS - GRADE: B+

Our long IPL nightmare is over. Test cricket has followed the lead of both Alf and skivvies in the pop cultural lexicon by being back!

Not only back, but back in one of the great time slots. I've said it before and I'll say it again: Winter evening Test cricket is among the best things ever invented. Great work on both a latitudinal and longitudinal front, England.

This time around, the geographically perfect England deigned to give Ireland a Test at Lord's, as we all began warming up for the Ashes. (Australia's warm-up match for the Ashes will, of course, be the World Test Championship final against India next week. So we all have our different little methods.)

My warm-up process? Looking up the term 'skivvy' to see if the 'skivvies are back' reference a couple of paragraphs back will be completely misconstrued by non-Australian readers. I'm delighted to report that it almost certainly will be.

### RED LEATHER, YELLOW LEATHER - GRADE: D-

As part of England's Ashes preparation, they axed both Jimmy Anderson and Ollie Robinson from their starting eleven, giving Josh Tongue a Test debut instead.

Typically wily stuff from the Brendon McCullum-Ben Stokes brain trust, who knew that the idiot press would get themselves all in a twist about the wordplay potential for the name Tongue, and look no further into any of the leadership duo's other brewing schemes. This would allow them to concoct all manner of madcap plans, with no fourth estate oversight.

For example, if any cricket journalist had bothered to check the facts, instead of getting bogged down asking ChatGPT for all the tongue-based phrases ('slip of the Tongue? ooh, that's promising'), they would have discovered that Anderson and Robinson hadn't been dropped after all. Instead, they were being rested from the side as a 'precaution'.

> **Dan Liebke** @LiebCricket · 14h
> Stokes such a good captain he'll burn a review to welcome a rookie into the fold. #ENGvIRE
> 
> ♡ 1    ↻    ♡ 9    ᴵᴵᴵ 1,722    ↑

Makes sense. And much like that bowling pair, I will also be left out of Australia's warm-up Test next week as a precaution.

### OBESE BONSAI TREES - GRADE: B-

Once the Test began, more seasoned observers of the game were able to look past the obvious trap of getting all worked up at the exciting prospect of Tongue puns. Instead, they focussed on the tried-and-true possibilities inherent in your Roots, your Potts and Popes. Or even your Ducketts and Leaches.

For example, Stuart Broad and Matthew Potts opened the bowling, allowing us all to think about broad pots for a bit. How could we make it work? Are broad pots wide cooking dishes used to boil particularly fat eggs - say an ostrich egg? Or do we go for the potted *plant* angle and muse instead on the breadth of the roots of some ghastly obese bonsai trees?

Loads of options. And that was just the opening bowling pair. What a sport Test cricket is.

Anyway, Ireland looked rickety early, with Broad threatening to go on one of his blitzes. He took four quick wickets, only one of which was cruelly overturned by the humourless ball-tracking.

The great fast bowler attempted to celebrate his burst of wickets with a Broadface, but even that was rusty this early in the Test match season, a half-hearted hand-in-the-vicinity-of-the-mouth thing.

No matter. He'll be right. By the time the Ashes roll around, and he blows away, say, Steve Smith, Marnus Labuschagne, Alex Carey and a stunningly recalled Shaun Marsh in the space of thirteen balls in the second Test, we'll get the proper thing. Something to look forward to, for sure.

❄

## MORPHEUS OFF THE SHORT RUN

Here's what I slept through in the rest of the day's play:

> *England continued to get themselves warm*
> *Bowling Ireland out cheaply, finding some form*
> *Then they gave it some tap,*
> *Closing the first innings gap*
> *At six runs an over, as per the new Bazball norm*

# DAY TWO

### GENERATIVE FILL TECHNOLOGY - GRADE: D

England resumed on the second day, using that new-fangled AI generative fill technology to extrapolate an entire day's play from yesterday's stumps scorecard.

Ben Duckett extrapolated his innings to the fastest ever 150 at Lord's, once again reducing Bradman to a laughable old fool, settling for sad silver.

Ollie Pope, meanwhile, extrapolated his innings to a double century before being stumped. In doing so, he matched Duckett's feat of scoring a hundred in a session (not to be mistaken, of course, for 'The Hundred' in *Succession*).

Yet despite their improbable feats, it still took England 35 overs to get a lead of 35. This, then, is the paradox of England's modern way of playing. A lot of thrashing and bashing for such a sluggish result. Once again, Bazball proves to be a sham.

## BUCKET HATS - GRADE: A-

Of course, Pope and Duckett's innings were mere extrapolations of the previous day's play.

The 'generative' portion that makes modern AI so fascinating only took root when, fittingly, Joe Root came out to bat. Predictably, the AI generated a score for him that almost precisely matched his average.

Then Harry Brook could only score 9* from 7 balls, as per recent IPL form and Jonny Bairstow did not bat, as per recent broken leg form. So the technology *seems* clever, but when you really dig into it, there's nothing that remarkable about it.

There's, therefore, still a place for humans in the modern cricketing world, as Stuart Broad demonstrated before play, doing an interview in an inexplicable bucket hat. Classic Broad nonsense, you might think. Then you look up to the dressing room and see pretty much the entire team in bucket hats, cheering on Duckett and Pope's cruel batting.

One can only assume that Rob Key ordered some extra hats for 'BDuckett', then somebody down at the ECB factory misread the order and now they all have to pretend like it's what they intended all along.

That's the kind of glorious mess that only a human can concoct. (For now, at least. Hat-misunderstanding technology is advancing rapidly!)

❄

DAN LIEBKE

## MORPHEUS OFF THE SHORT RUN

Here's what I slept through in the rest of the day's play:

*England's run-a-ball 500 earned fawning praise*
*Declaring just after tea, no further delays*
*The golf course, it beckoned,*
*And Stokes mistakenly reckoned*
*They could win the Test in just a couple of days*

# DAY THREE

### EFFECTIVENESS - GRADE: A

Ireland began the day three wickets down, but *effectively* four wickets down with the injury to James McCollum that ensured he would not bat again.

Still 255 runs behind, this opened the door for Ireland to achieve a rare *double-effectively* should they be able to close the run gap.

Harry Tector and Lorcan Tucker were the first to embrace this mad dream, putting on a 63-run partnership. An impressive effort, even if Tucker and Tector sounds like some kind of horrifically dangerous 18th century factory machinery.

"Oi, what happened to Jimmy's arm?"

"Ooh. Terrible story. It got trapped in the tucker-and-tector. Torn off at the wrist. Grisly stuff."

Even when those two were dismissed, Ireland stuck to their goal, with Andy McBrine and Mark Adair adding 163 runs in rapid time.

It was enough to get Ireland within range of England, and a mighty blow from number eleven Graham Hume took the visitors to 8/353. Or, *effectively* 9 for *effectively* 1 (or *effectively* 1 for *effectively* 9 if you score in the non-Australian way).

An *effectively* beautiful moment.

### CORRECTLY SPELLING WORDS - GRADE: A-

Ireland's last pair then batted their way to a delayed tea break, forcing everybody to sit around for twenty minutes in the dressing room, contemplating what was the point of any of it.

Shortly after the delayed tea, Ireland's final wicket fell, setting England eleven runs to win. Zak Crawley obnoxiously knocked off the target in four balls and that was that.

A grand triumph for England, with plenty of positives to bask in heading into the Ashes.

Josh Tongue finished with five wickets in the second innings and looks to be not just a bright prospect for England but also a boon to the dream of more people learning how to spell 'tongue' with the 'u' in the correct place. (Similarly, I would very much like to see a Josh Lose enter the international cricket (and accurate spelling) scene ASAP.)

Ben Stokes had a fine captain's Test. Didn't bat. Didn't bowl. But did wave his batters in at one point. Also caught a ball and winced in pain. A genuine all-rounder.

On the negative side, Duckett struggled to get going in the second innings. His consistency will be a concern. Still, that's Bazball for you.

> **Dan Liebke** @LiebCricket · 14h
> I mostly feel sorry for fans from other nations who are now left in the unpleasant bind of feeling as if they have to support Australia during the Ashes so that they don't have to listen to smug Bazball evangelism for cricketing eternity.
>
> It should never come to that.
>
> ♡ 5   ⟲ 6   ♡ 36   ıll 5,320   ⏏

# WORLD TEST CHAMPIONSHIP FINAL

# AUSTRALIA V INDIA

THE OVAL, LONDON

# DAY ONE

## SWAGGERING BRAVADO - GRADE: C

Australia's warm-up for the Ashes and India's warm-down from the IPL continues with the World Test Championship Final, a contest to determine once and for all, which is the greatest Test cricket nation. (By 'once', I mean 'it happened previously, but New Zealand won it, so we should probably just ignore that' and by 'for all', I mean 'the entire idea could well be killed off by the ICC in favour of, I dunno, a second T20 World Cup so whoever wins this one may hold the mace-trophy in perpetuity'.)

India strutted to the middle of the Oval, full of intimidatory tactics. They omitted the number one Test ranked bowler, Ravi Ashwin, from their starting eleven. Presumably as an act of swaggering bravado (bravido? No). *Don't even need the best bowler in this format to beat you lot*, they were saying. Magnificent stuff.

Then Mohammed Siraj had Usman Khawaja, Australia's most prolific batter during the two-year qualifying period, out without adding to that prolificacy. *Think you're all that, Ussie? Well, you're not.*

And when the number one ranked Test batter, Marnus Labuschagne, made his way to the crease, India also treated him with scandalous disrespect. Not only did they hit him on the thumb twice (superb accuracy from the India bowlers), they also reviewed him twice for LBW, with Rohit Sharma indulging in a stretched out, behind-the-back, T-sign. Quite literally, a flex from the India captain.

> **Dan Liebke** @LiebCricket · 12h
> Physiotherapist gives Marnus the thumbs up to continue batting.
> #WTCFinal
> 
> 💬 2   🔁   ♡ 28   📊 2,136   ⬆

## SODDIN' BAZBALL - GRADE: D

India's in-your-face domination saw Labuschagne and David Warner struggle to just 22 runs in the first ten overs.

22 runs in 10 overs?! The English public must have been ready to storm the ground in apoplectic fury. "Where's me soddin' Bazball!" they cried. "I didn't pay sixty quid to watch 2.2 runs per bloomin' over." (Pretty sure I've nailed the accent there.)

The dominance of ball over bat couldn't last, however. Australia had correctly assessed that, because of India's IPL-centric preparation, they would only have twenty overs of high-intensity cricket in them for the innings. And so it proved, despite both Warner and Labuschagne falling on either side of lunch. (Not literally 'falling'. They just lost their wickets, and walked off, heroically upright.)

Of course, because of India's sluggish first session over rate, those twenty overs did take us more or less to the lunch break.

Question: How many points do India need to lose to a slow over rate for South Africa to be subbed in halfway through the Test?

## CLARIFYING THE SIMPSONS - GRADE: F

Of course, during the lunch break, Channel Seven showed us football chat. Forty minutes to fill. Can't possibly do it by talking about the sport you've flown to the other side of the planet to cover.

James Brayshaw, a man who'd started the broadcast by shouting at me about grand finals and players being 'up for it', and former Australian cricketer, coach and janitor Justin Langer initiated an impromptu Algonquin Round Table with a football boofhead who I think they were calling 'the Trash Compactor' (?). I have no idea why.

> **Dan Liebke** @LiebCricket · 9h
> Imagine if you were the cricketing idiot that Matt Hayden is imagining he's talking to. An honour in a way. #WTCFinal
> ○ 3   ⟳   ♡ 24   ‖ 2,020   ↑

What an enormously frustrating way to make the already frustrating longest break in the day's play feel even longer.

To reinterpret and clarify the famous Simpsons' quote: "When cricket's not on screen, all the commentators should *not* be asking 'where's football?'".

## SOLVING PROBLEMS - GRADE: A

After Mohammed Shami bowled Labuschagne shortly after lunch (cue a reinterpreted and clarified quote from the other great 1990s comedy show, *Seinfeld*: "That's a Shami."), Travis Head arrived at the crease.

He and Steve Smith then put on an unbeaten 251 run partnership to take Australia to stumps with the score 327/3. Head scored 146* from 156 balls in a typically thrilling and terrifying knock. Watching Head bat in this manner *is* fun. I can see why having a team full of such lunatics must be so exhilarating for England fans. On the other Head, having more than one of them going at a time might just do me in.

Fun, yes. But fun in the way that surviving a home-made rocket launch is fun.

Which is why the far more sedate innings of Steve Smith was appreciated. During the innings, Smith's head popped up on screen at one point and told us all how he liked 'solving problems' while out in the middle.

A bowler will come at him with Goldbach's conjecture and he'll cobble together a proof. A close fielder might throw forth the Riemann hypothesis from under the lid, and he'll provide a counterexample. Fermat? Easy. Just scribble a proof in the margin of the scorecard. Plenty of room.

Classic Smith. He's 95* from 227 balls. No problem.

# DAY TWO

## PACKED OCTOBER CALENDARS - GRADE: A-

Steve Smith and Travis Head picked up on day two from where they left off on day one, as they are required to do, not just by historical convention, but by the very laws of the game. You can't just skip a few overs to get your eye in, or go back and have some do-overs of that tricky mini-session just before stumps. No. Continuity is sacrosanct, and just one of the many aspects of Test cricket that we traditionalists savour.

It therefore made sense that Smith followed up his last-ball four on the first day, with a pair of fours from his first two balls on the second to bring up his 31st Test century. As an indicator of how impressive a feat this is, think of it as one Test century for every day in October - a month in which Australia traditionally plays little to no Test cricket! Astonishing. (How does he find time to make a Halloween costume?) Now, he just needs to put his head down and knock off the other months.

Can he do it? Certainly, Matthew Hayden in commentary believes he can. I say that with some certainty, because Hayden believes in a lot of things, boldly predicting that both Smith and Head would go on to reach double centuries when Smith was on just 106.

> **Dan Liebke** @LiebCricket · 11h
> I think my favourite quality of Hayden's commentary is his confidence in my abilities. "He runs between the wickets hard, as all Australians do." "He pulls the short ball well, as all Australians do." I hope someday I can reward his faith in me. #WTCFinal
>
> 💬 7    🔁 2    ♡ 119    ııl 4,997    ⬆

Smith was described as batting inside his 'bubble', a reference to how he doesn't allow outside influences to affect his concentration. A reasonable enough descriptor back in 2019, when Australia last toured England, but surely one that can be supplanted in 2023. After all, in late 2021, Smith was infamously trapped in an elevator, relying on Marnus to slip him M&Ms through a crack in the door to survive. I say, commemorate that wonderful moment by replacing all tired references to Steve Smith batting in a 'bubble' with modern allusions to him instead batting in an 'elevator'.

Unluckily for Hayden, Smith was dismissed for a shameful 121 (a base 11 ton, to you and me), playing on to Shardul Thakur. Head, for his part, stumbled on 163.

When are we going to have a conversation as a cricket nation about Travis Head's inability to convert 150s to 200s?

## SEDUCTIVE FIENDS - GRADE: C-

The wickets of Head and Smith allowed India to drag themselves back into the match. Cameron Green bounded to the middle, playing joyously like the enormous puppy he is, unable to be caught (until he was, by Shubman Gill at slip).

Alex Carey, meanwhile, came to the crease under grave accusations from the television graphic that he 'likes to manipulate field'. One imagines he gaslights the slips cordon. Uses reverse psychology on the men in the deep. Employs over-the-top flattery on the rest. A wily and seductive fiend.

But it wasn't just Carey indulging in mind games. When it was Mitchell Starc's turn to bat, he played and missed at several balls before drilling it straight to substitute fielder Axar Patel and running himself out. Knew he was about to edge one behind at any moment. Took the tactical option of not giving the wicket to the bowler. Great mind games from the left arm quick.

## FAKE TS- GRADE: A

India wrapped up the Australian innings for 469 during the middle session. A good fightback, after Australia dominated the first day.

The highlight of India's day two recovery? Captain Rohit Sharma's employment of a fake T signal.

While pondering a review, Rohit moved one hand at right angles above the other, seemingly in preparation to call for DRS. However, and this is crucial, the top hand at no point touched the bisecting lower hand, instead hovering sultrily above it.

This was highly confusing to both the umpires and Australian batters, as one might imagine. But imagine how much more confusing it could be. How close can he get his hands together without touching? Will there soon be an umpire's review to determine if Rohit asked for a player's review? God, I hope so.

A superb innovation from the India skipper, to go with his splendid behind-the-back T-making on day one. Cummins must feel like a fool to be so emphatically outplayed by his counterpart in this area.

Oh, sure, Cummins dismissed Rohit, plumb LBW when India came out to bat for just 14. So plumb, in fact, that Rohit didn't even bother making a fake T. Still, cold comfort for Australia's captain.

※

DAN LIEBKE

MORPHEUS OFF THE SHORT RUN

Here's what I slept through in the rest of the day's play:

>*After Pat Cummins got Rohit with a peach*
>*Shubman Gill, Boland was able to breach*
>*Pujara was then out to Green,*
>*Starc got Kohli for only fourteen*
>*And Jadeja to Lyon, to give the bowlers one each*

# DAY THREE

## DEALING WITH TRUCK DINER BULLIES - GRADE: D

Australia arrived at The Oval on the third day, keen to wrap up the India first innings and mount an insurmountable lead.

Scott Boland took a wicket with his second ball to set that plan in efficient motion. Pat Cummins then began roughing up Shardul Thakur, in a manner that looked for all the world like that scene at the end of *Superman 2*, where Supes teaches that random truck diner bully a valuable lesson by throwing him into a pinball machine. Ha ha ha! Take that, ya stupid bully!

In the case of Cummins, with no pinball machine in immediate proximity, that meant instead peppering the number eight with balls that struck him painfully on the hand and forearm. Get ready for a broken Thakur arm.

Cummins' cruel intimidation worked perfectly, with Thakur squeezing an edge to Cameron Green at gully. I remain a big fan of

DAN LIEBKE

Australia fielding three gullies to this India batting lineup in the form of Green's nonsense wingspan.

Alas, Green's wingspan didn't help him this time, as the ball went in and out of his enormous, grasping hands. Get somebody taller in, I say.

## BAGGY GREEN WHEELS - GRADE: D

At first, everybody assumed Thakur would be furious at Green for dropping the chance and keeping him in the Cummins firing line. Instead, however, the missed grab proved a turning point with Thakur and Ajinkya Rahane putting on a century stand together to drag India within eight runs of an irrelevant follow-on mark.

The Australian fielding wheels fell completely off in the partnership's wake, raising the important question: Should they have even been allowed wheels in such an important match in the first place? Once again, the hard-nosed Aussies pushing the line of fair play.

Without their baggy green wheels, catches were dropped, wickets were undone due to the overstepping skipper, and reviews were burnt on non-existent edges. (Although, to be fair, the last one seemed mostly an attempt from the slips cordon to have the third umpire prove that Cummins' front foot was behind the crease for at least one delivery. Great show of support for the skipper.)

The lunch break gave Australia an opportunity to reattach their wheels. Having done so, they proceeded to swiftly take the final four wickets after lunch, beginning with Green plucking an absurd catch from behind his formidable head to dismiss Rahane.

> Dan Liebke @LiebCricket · 11h
> Hayden describes Green's catch via a metaphor based on something almost nobody has ever seen. A wild ploy. Classic Haydos. #WTCFinal
> ♡ 1    ⟲ 2    ♡ 25    ᴵ|ᴵ 2,716    ⬆

When Green trapped number eleven Mohammed Siraj a few overs later, India were all out for 294 and the Australians started running off the ground to prepare for their second innings. Only to have to run back *on* the ground when the seemingly desperate review that was taken only because India had one remaining turned out to be valid.

"We have a clear spike on UltraEdge. Australia, I'll need you to reverse your departure to the dressing room. You're on screen now."

※

## MORPHEUS OFF THE SHORT RUN

Here's what I slept through in the rest of the day's play:

> *Smith and Marnus together, movers and shakers*
> *Comfortably negating strange bounce and pitch breakers*
> *Then Ravindra Jadeja*
> *Conjured something major*
> *And dismissed both first innings ton-makers*

# DAY FOUR

### CAMERON GREEN'S PADS - GRADE: F

Australia lost Marnus Labuschagne early on the first day. Not just his wicket, but Marnus himself, as the eccentric number three was last seen sleepwalking out of the dressing room and into a nearby sewer drain where he was presumably devoured by an evil clown who lives under London. That clown's name? (Insert local political satire here.)

The loss of Labuschagne had Australia in trouble. Yes, they were still well ahead of the game, but the innings desperately needed to be regenerated if they were to push the fourth innings run chase beyond India's reach.

Luckily, basic Anagram Theory teaches us that if you need *regeneracy*, that's when you call in *Green-Carey*.

The pair slowly but surely put a partnership together. With the emphasis on the 'slowly' part, particularly for Cameron Green, who made his way to a stodgy 25 (95) before trying to pad Ravindra Jadeja away, only for the ball to deflect back onto his stumps.

# WORLD TEST CHAMPIONSHIP FINAL

The lesson is clear. After all, if Cameron Green can't pad a ball away successfully, can anybody? (Explanation of joke: Green's pads are very big. Because he's tall.)

Hopefully Green practises his padding away a bit more at next year's IPL. That's where those kinds of skills are best honed.

## CAMERON GREEN'S FINGERS - GRADE: A

Pat Cummins' declaration at 8/270 set India 444 to win. The target meant that all four umpires began the innings with one leg off the ground. A lovely nod to the memory of David Shepherd.

> **Dan Liebke** @LiebCricket · 12h
> Cummins sees Rohit's fake review and raises him a fake declaration.
> #WTCFinal
> ♡ 1   ⟲   ♡ 18   ᴵᴵᴵ 1,677   ⬆

A less lovely nod, at least from the perspective of India fans, came when the freewheeling start to the innings by Shubman Gill and Rohit Sharma was ended by third umpire Richard Kettleborough's decision to say 'yes' to an appeal for a low catch from Cameron Green.

You can see why the India fans thought it was not out. After all, replay after replay showed clear signs of Green in contact with the red ball. But this was not enough to sway Kettleborough in Gill's favour.

The decision enraged India supporters at the ground. (The ones on social media were predictably chill about it, of course. 'The umpire's decision is final,' was the sanguine consensus online. 'A shame for Gill, obviously, but sometimes the breaks don't go your way,' offered other passionate fans. 'A tight call and therefore ultimately one best left to a neutral, highly skilled umpire,' suggested the rest. Elon Musk's Twitter, as ever, a haven for common sense and nuanced discussion.)

At the ground, however, the India fans began chanting 'cheat' at Cameron Green, eliciting a tiny tear from the enormous puppy dog cricketer. As the song goes, 'It's Not Easy Being Green (And Being

Called A Cheat By Enraged Fans Of The Opposition For Appealing For A Low Catch That The Third Umpire Then Confirms That You Have Caught)'. Boy, Kermit fucken *nailed* that.

Everything was anti-climax after the wicket of Gill. Sure, Rohit Sharma was LBW trying to sweep Nathan Lyon. Best bit of that dismissal was Steve Smith sprinting from first slip towards leg slip to try to take a catch and then screeching to a cartoon character halt behind Carey to appeal. Good stuff.

Shortly after, Cheteshwar Pujara responded to a short ball from Cummins by dinking an upper-cut straight through to Carey. Given that Ben Stokes has outlawed the use of the phrase 'bad shot' for the next several weeks, I have no further comment to make about Pujara's effort.

But with 280 runs needed on the final day, Virat Kohli and Ajinkya Rahane still at the crease, India remain a chance to pull off a stunning victory. Particularly with Shubman Gill apparently due to return to the crease after a truly heroic campaign of overnight social media sulking.

# DAY FIVE

## MARNUS LABUSCHAGNE'S UNRELIABLE PRECOGNITION - GRADE: C-

India's prospects of completing a world record fourth innings run chase were brought predictably undone by Scott Boland, a great Australian who cares about what time we all get to go to bed.

In fact, so predictable was Boland's breakthrough that Marnus Labuschagne heard Virat Kohli's edge to a diving Steve Smith at slip *two balls* before it happened. Amazing. But not as amazing as him somehow being able to convince Pat Cummins to review it. Come on, Pat. You know we never listen to Marnus. His precognition is all over the place.

## GOING VIRAL - GRADE: B

With Kohli gone, and Ravindra Jadeja following two balls later, the match was over. Mitchell Starc and Nathan Lyon cleaned up the tail, and that was that. Australia were World Test Champions by 209 runs, prompting truly outlandish jingoistic nonsense from Matthew Hayden. Somebody please stuff a baggy green in that man's mouth.

Travis Head was named player of the match for his thrashing around back on the first day. A bit of a disappointing decision for mine. I would have given it to Cameron Green, who didn't confine his heroics to just the one day but who had the entire cricketing world talking *throughout* the Test.

Heck, he even came up with a ridiculous, bungled padding-away dismissal that nobody is even discussing any more, because he's conjured an even more viral wicket since. Great social media management from the giant puppy.

Instead, Green had to settle for a mere winner's medal alongside the rest of his less blowing-up-on-the-internet team mates. I feel bad for the dude who had to put the medal over his head. (Explanation: because he's so tall.)

# THE MEN'S ASHES

9 FEB 2023 - 13 MAR 2023

# FIRST TEST

## EDGBASTON, BIRMINGHAM

# DAY ONE

## MARKING RUN-UPS - GRADE: A

The first Ashes Test began with some magnificent trolling from Mitch Marsh, who, for reasons known only to himself, began marking his run-up shortly after Scott Boland had marked his and before there'd been any appearance from either Josh Hazlewood or Mitchell Starc.

Marsh's efforts swiftly had everybody at the ground in a dither. Were Australia playing *two* all-rounders? Were *both* Hazlewood and Starc missing the first Test? Was this a return to the classic Mitches and Marshes era of Australian cricket but with just the one cricketer embodying all such roles?

Alas, no. Hazlewood eventually showed up to mark his run-up and put an end to all the nonsense, and we settled instead for *zero* cricketers in either the Mitch or Marsh (or Mitch Marsh) roles.

Nevertheless, a good comic bit from Mitch Marsh, who was last seen hacking the Cricket Australia website and running his mark-up.

(A <small> HTML gag </small> there for all the nerds.)

DAN LIEBKE

## OVERCORDIALED TODDLERS - GRADE: C-

The absence of Starc meant that he was incredibly unlikely to dismiss Rory Burns first ball of this series, as he did in the previous one. A chance made even slimmer by Burns' ongoing non-selection in the England side. It's on these 'one-percenters' that the entire Ashes might turn.

Instead of Burns, England continue to persevere with Zak Crawley. He crashed a four from Pat Cummins' first ball, setting an entirely different tone for this series.

Or did it? Because as the session stretched out, the Australians' game plan became clear. They would let Crawley - and the rest of the frenetic England batting line-up - thrash and smash like overcordialed toddlers, wait for them to tucker themselves out and *then* pick up their wickets. Heck, they wouldn't even appeal for one of Crawley's edges, so committed were they to letting him exhaust himself.

The plan worked perfectly in the first session, as Australia took three wickets on a flat batting track. This, despite the consternation of several England journalists (and Mark Taylor), overcome with the vapours at the sight of Australia having fielders in the deep, like this was the boring middle overs of an ODI.

> **Dan Liebke** @LiebCricket · 15h
> Long time without Channel Nine cricket coverage but Mark Taylor has just sold Travis Head a Fujitsu air conditioner, so fair to say he's still got it.
> #Ashes
> ◯ 3   ⟲ 2   ♡ 111   ıl 7,006   ⇪

'Yes,' the England press (and Tubby) sneered. 'Australia have edged ahead of England in the first session, but at what cost? If the cowardly Cummins is going to position fielders to cut off England's god-given right to hit boundaries, then why do we even play this game?'

## CRUMBLING EDIFICES - GRADE: B-

In the second session, Harry Brook and Joe Root looked to take the innings away from Australia. And when Travis Head - definitively *not* the number three ranked fielder in the world - dropped the hyper-aggressive Brook in the outfield, alarm bells were ringing.

Unfortunately, those alarm bells seemed to throw off *Brook* rather than the Australians. First, he played out the innings' first maiden, before following it up by losing his wicket to a Nathan Lyon mystery ball that deflected off Brook's bat, into the sky, between baffled close-in Australian fielders, onto the back of Brook's legs, before finally crashing into the stumps. Tremendous accuracy from Lyon. When Ben Stokes edged behind almost immediately after that, England were 176/5 and the entire Bazball edifice was crumbling.

Fortunately for England, however, Jonny Bairstow, a registered structural engineer, arrived at the crease next to join Joe Root to conduct some edifice repair and see England safely to tea.

❋

## MORPHEUS OFF THE SHORT RUN

Here's what I slept through in the rest of the day's play:

> *Another fine Bazball counter-attack*
> *Jonny and Joe giving it a jolly good whack*
> *Then some Stokes inspiration.*
> *A surprise declaration!*
> *To ensure Dave Warner was cut zero slack*

# DAY TWO

## ENGAGEMENT PARTIES - GRADE: F

With the match evenly poised after the first day, following England's bold deployment of Bazball, it was annoying to miss most of the first session of the second day, due to required attendance at an engagement party. Young love truly is a ghastly thing.

Although perhaps missing the session was not as annoying as it might have been, given Steve Smith's dogged determination to pursue the very opposite of Bazball - Llabzab, presumably - in scoring a tedious, boundaryless 16 (59), before Ben Stokes thankfully got rid of him.

Smith, of course, had arrived at the crease after Stuart Broad dismissed David Warner and Marnus Labuschagne in consecutive balls, the former for the *fifteenth* time in Tests.

Has dismissing Warner become a mental crutch for Broad? Sadly, this seems to be the case.

## OAFISH MITTS - GRADE: C+

The middle session then saw Travis Head and Usman Khawaja rebuild the Australian innings by the recommended method of smashing Moeen Ali for as many boundaries as possible.

However, just as we began to ruminate about how brave it was for England to go into the Test without a spinner, Head chipped Moeen straight to Zak Crawley at mid-wicket.

When Cameron Green then came down the pitch two balls later and was beaten in flight for an easy stumping, the cocky Australian reports of England's spinnerlessness proved to be greatly exaggerated.

The reports of England's keeperlessness, however? Well, they're still alive and awkwardly fumbling run-of-the-mill stumping opportunities. For Jonny Bairstow not only missed the chance to dismiss Green but later botched several other chances with his clumsy, oafish mitts.

Having seen Bairstow bat brilliantly last year, I'm begrudgingly willing to accept the prospect of having to now take him seriously as a batter, as improbable as that feels. It's a relief, then, that we still don't have to take him seriously as a keeper.

❊

## MORPHEUS OFF THE SHORT RUN

Here's what I slept through in the rest of the day's play:

> *Khawaja cruising to an imperious ton*
> *Sweater-adorned, despite English sun*
> *Ignoring the wickets tumbling*
> *And Bairstow's crude bumbling*
> *But still letting Broad bowl him for some grand no ball fun*

# DAY THREE

## GALAGA BONUS STAGES - GRADE: B+

Australia began the day with high hopes of taking a first innings lead, particularly with Usman Khawaja anchoring the innings brilliantly.

Although, not, of course, as brilliantly as Jonny Bairstow, who dropped yet another chance that came his way early in the morning. Between the combined efforts of Khawaja and Bairstow, there seemed to be no way England could take the final five wickets to fall.

> **Dan Liebke** @LiebCricket · 14h
> Ben Stokes claps his hands twice and his ruthless team all move into their predetermined fielding positions. #Ashes
> 💬 2   🔁   ♡ 25   ᶥᶥᶩ 3,199   ⬆

Then, suddenly, Ben Stokes decided to pull one of his silly buggers pieces of captaincy, employing a field that looked like a screenshot from a *Galaga* bonus stage. Amazingly, despite that outdated reference point, the tactic worked, a bemused Khawaja playing all around a delivery from Ollie Robinson and having his stumps rattled.

Is funny cricket captaincy identical to good cricket captaincy? All signs point to yes.

## BATHING IN KOOL-AID - GRADE: C-

The wicket of Khawaja sent commentators Kevin Pietersen and Eoin Morgan into fits of delight. Not content with drinking the Bazball Kool-Aid, the pair were utterly bathing in it, pouring it over one another with giant jugs as they chortled and cheered for all their might as England took the last four wickets to fall for a mere fourteen runs.

Of course, there is nothing unusual about partisanship in a commentary box during an Ashes series. However, Pietersen losing his mind at England's 'brilliant' plan to bring undone the batting powerhouse that is Scott Boland (Test batting average 4.50) was top tier work that would have sat proudly alongside the very best of the one-eyed Channel Nine stuff.

And yet somehow this commentary was less annoying than the middle session of the previous day when, after two hours of listening to the commentators endlessly praise Stokes' wily and brilliant captaincy and his courageous fields (in contrast to the cowardly, tentative Australians), those same commentators then sent us to tea by declaring it 'Australia's session'.

Come on, guys. At least give us a hint.

## PRE-EMPTIVE DECLARATIONS - GRADE: C

After the first ball of the second innings, England were *seven* runs ahead of Australia. A 75% improvement on their effort from the first ball of the first innings. Marvellous stuff from Zak Crawley, whose rate of development is staggering.

Ha ha ha! But no, of course not. Crawley played out a shameful dot ball first up, and the seven run lead was, in fact, a result of the first innings totals, in which England, despite declaring eight wickets down, still outscored their great rivals.

Although, having said that, in a way, didn't Australia declare eight down first by selecting three number elevens in their line-up? Makes you think.

Before too long, however, the rain began to fall. The drops soon went all Jonny Bairstow on us, growing too numerous and relentless to be ignored. The umpires took the players off, and despite the deployment of the same drying agent that saw Moeen Ali cruelly fined in his return to Test cricket, there was only time for Australia to take the cheap wickets of both openers before the rest of the day was washed out.

# DAY FOUR

## FIRST BALL REVERSE SCOOPS - GRADE: A

After much of the previous day's play was rained out, the fourth day was extended. However, in another typically childish display from the ECB, the extra time was added to the end of the day's play, when it was 4am for Australian viewers back home, rather than the beginning of the day when it's 7:30pm. Easily the most disgraceful act of the Ashes so far.

Nevertheless, England, in the impish form of Joe Root, began the day in typically nonsensical fashion, apparently planning to declare in the first half hour of the day, as he tried to reverse-scoop Pat Cummins for six first ball. Sure, it didn't work, but he had the idea to do it and the willingness to attempt it, no matter how crazy it might seem to the naysayers and the establishment squares. And that's what Bazball is all about.

## NEAR-SPOONERISED AWKWARDNESS - GRADE: C

Another thing Bazball is apparently all about it? Randomly running down the pitch at Nathan Lyon and being stumped. So Joe Root did that too, but not until he'd made 46.

Seeing Alex Carey glove the chance so effortlessly must have made for uncomfortable viewing for both the man with the ball-resisting fingers, Jonny Bairstow (who demonstrated his commitment to the 'balls bouncing off his gloves' bit so thoroughly that he allowed it to also happen while batting and scurrying through for a quick single) and the man with the raw-blistering fingers, Moeen Ali (who later came out to bat, to the cruel taunts of the knowledgeable Edgbaston crowd waving drying agent at him).

But the near-spoonerised awkwardness didn't deter either of them from making a modest contribution. Indeed, despite no England batter *really* getting going, every single one of them contributed between ten and fifty runs (obvious exception: Zak Crawley), as England scrambled their way to 273 all out.

It meant Australia needed 281 to win, a run chase that I can now exclusively reveal is of a similar magnitude to a previous run chase.

How did England start their defence of this total? By asking for the ball to be changed before a single delivery was bowled.

Bazball, baby!

## MORPHEUS OFF THE SHORT RUN

Here's what I slept through in the rest of the day's play:

> *A monumental tussle, one of the great Test matches*
> *With each team taking turns for dominant patches*
> *Until Broad's new outswinger myth*
> *Found the bats of Marnus and Smith*
> *And Bairstow improbably hung onto the catches*

# DAY FIVE

## BEN STOKES' BOLLOCKS - GRADE: A

After the first session of the final day was lost to criminal England rain, Scott Boland and Usman Khawaja resumed for Australia. A glimpse of Australia's openers for the second Test? Perhaps.

Australia needed 174 further runs to win as play commenced, with England requiring seven more wickets. Boland was the first to fall, yet again caught behind by the safe gloves of Jonny Bairstow. Wild to think that at that point, Bairstow had taken the first four catches of the innings and yet dropped fewer than ten.

Travis Head was then swiftly spun out by Moeen Ali's blistered finger, and Cameron Green offered a chance early, squeezing an edge just wide of first slip to a position where he would have been dazzlingly caught by Cameron Green had he been fielding. (A big mistake from England *not* to have him fielding, if I'm being honest. A surprising lack of Bazball imagination in this instance.)

And yet, despite the relative flakiness of every other batter, Khawaja remained ever-present, a man who had batted not just on every day of this Test match but through the entirety of living memory. As long as he remained at the crease, Australia remained a chance.

So, of course, Ben Stokes brought himself on and golden-bollocksed Khawaja out, spurred on by the frenetic Edgbaston crowd.

This shameful England team once again blatantly drawing on performance-enhancing crowd support. The ICC needs to step in.

RIGHTEOUS REPUDIATIONS - GRADE: D

With Khawaja out, Bairstow was now the man most likely to get Australia home. Did his clumsy hands have one more relieving drop in them?

No, as it turned out. But it did appear as if he'd offered some catching practice to Joe Root, who dropped return chances from Alex Carey twice, before hanging onto his third opportunity. If at first (and second) you don't get caught by Joe Root, driving one straight back at him, try, try again, is the Carey credo.

And that was that. 54 runs still needed, with Nathan Lyon joining Pat Cummins in the middle. Now only a matter of time until Australia's last pair of number elevens were prised out by England's bowler.

A superb victory for England, testament to the healing power of Bazball, and a righteous repudiation of Australia's gormless brand of cricket. At least, that was the verdict according to Kevin Pietersen (and inexplicable 'kick this Australian side' sidekick Kumar Sangakkara). It was frankly amazing that Cummins' hapless team of spineless idiots had got as close as they had, given the absolute litany of cowardly and foolhardy errors the commentators had spent the entire Test assuring me they'd been making.

(For the record, Bazball itself is amazing and thrilling and fun and helped make this one of the truly great Tests. It's just the commentators' endless proselytising and/or condemnation of cricket heathens yet to see the Stokesian light that grows a tad tiresome after the first twelve or thirteen hours. I mean, it's four am, guys. We've got religious programming just a remote control channel change away if we really wanted to listen to that.)

## PAT FUCKEN CUMMINS - GRADE: A+

And yet... Cummins had apparently not been listening to Pietersen and his fellow preachers, proving yet again he is the wisest and handsomest of us all. For instead the Australian captain brutally at first, then sensibly later, guided his team safely to victory, finishing on 44 not out.

No sweat. Cummins has been doing this kind of thing since literally his teenaged debut.

> **Dan Liebke** @LiebCricket · 8h
> I'm old enough to remember when Zak Crawley's boundary off the first ball was going to set the tone for the entire #Ashes
> ♡ 7   ↻ 82   ♡ 1,229   ıll 42.2K   ⬆

A brilliant Test that swayed thrillingly back and forth between the two sides. Yes, we all had a laugh at Broad's wonderfully mental comments about the previous Ashes series being void. But it's also reasonable to point out that this one match contained more excitement than that entire prior series.

It's fun when England don't give up at the first sign of a challenge. They should do it more often.

# SECOND TEST

## LORD'S, LONDON

# DAY ONE

### CLIMATE CHANGE PROTESTS - GRADE: A

The opening of the second Test was interrupted by Just Stop Oil protests, as members of the environmental activist group somehow invaded the ground to release orange powder onto the wicket.

They had not, however, reckoned with the counter-ploy of the orangest man in world cricket, Jonny Bairstow. The England wicket-keeper responded to the invasion with typical pragmatism, simply picking up one of the protesters, lodging him beneath his arms and carrying him off the ground.

It was a surprise to see the protesters so curiously defensive against Bairstow, who made all the running in the incident. Were they rattled by his willingness to take the protest to them? You'd have to say yes.

Mostly, however, I was just disappointed that Pat Cummins didn't carry the protester immediately back on.

DAN LIEBKE

## OVER RATE OBFUSCATION - GRADE: C

The first session was therefore obviously Bairstow's. But, also, Australia's, who had openers Usman Khawaja and David Warner survive almost until lunch.

This was despite dark, overhead clouds that twice saw players forced from the ground for a brief rain delay, much to the annoyance of those of us back in Australia, trying desperately to stay awake. In fact, I speak for all Australians and/or environmental protesters in saying: "Sort your climate out, England."

Still, clever of England to have random weather/protester delays in a bid to obfuscate yet again another dreadful over rate.

Even when Khawaja (bowled not playing a shot) and Warner (bowled missing a shot) were dismissed either side of lunch to Josh Tongue, Marnus Labuschagne and Steve Smith came together to put the heat back on England.

> **Dan Liebke** @LiebCricket · 11h
> Smith fully infected with the Bazball mind virus. Will be playing for England in the second innings. #Ashes
> 💬   🔁   ♡ 25   ᐧ|ᐧ 1,640   ⤴

Smith swiftly brought up 9000 Test runs (the vast majority of them scored in this middle session) and the pair drove Stuart Broad, in particular, into a very grumpy mood. Broad had each of the prolific pair dismissed, only for them both to successfully overturn the decision via DRS.

> **Dan Liebke** @LiebCricket · 10h
> Grumpy Broad is one of my favourite brands of Broad. #Ashes
> 💬 1   🔁   ♡ 26   ᐧ|ᐧ 1,920   ⤴

# THE MEN'S ASHES

Maddening stuff for Broad, and presumably a promo for Channel Nine's new upcoming show.

> **Dan Liebke** @LiebCricket · 12h
> I often criticise their coverage, but genuinely grateful to Nine for warning us in advance that after the break "Kevin Pietersen joins us live". #Ashes
> ○ 8   ⟲ 15   ♡ 436   ᴵᴵᴵ 25.1K   ⬆

**NEXT WEEK ON NINE:** *The New Longest Feud: Broad v DRS*

❄

## MORPHEUS OFF THE SHORT RUN

Here's what I slept through in the rest of the day's play:

> *A moment of true wordplay dread*
> *During the innings of wee Travis Head*
> *Facing Josh Tongue*
> *(Albeit pronouncing it wrong)*
> *Made me thankful I was settled in bed*

# DAY TWO

## AUSTRALIA'S BEST BATTER - GRADE: A

Despite losing Alex Carey early on the second day (possibly carried away to a hidden location by wicket-keeping counterpart, Jonny Bairstow), Steve Smith continued to purr along to his century, aided by Ben Stokes' willingness to give him a single and attack the other end. (The purring, by the way, is yet another weird idiosyncrasy for Smith to add to his repertoire.)

> **Dan Liebke** @LiebCricket · 19h
> "This is not negative! this is not negative", kp continues to insist as he slowly shrinks and transforms into a corn cob.
> ♡ 2   ⟲ 4   ♡ 72   ᴵᴵᴵ 6,505   ⬆

Alongside his captain Pat Cummins, Smith brought up his 32nd Test century, matching Steve Waugh in approximately several hundred fewer innings. He now has just Ricky Ponting (41 Test centuries) as the only Australian batter ahead of him.

I'm not sure I'll ever fully understand Smith's transition from 'youngster selected to crack jokes in the dressing room' to 'all-time batting great who embodies humourless destruction.' To be frank, it's very weird.

Still, if he catches Ponting, that's going to be one heck of a final few years of his career.

At 7/393, though, Smith fell into one of Bazball's more subtle traps. In the first Test, Ben Stokes had declared on 8/393, perhaps setting in Steve Smith's mind the idea that this was the new done thing. As we all know by now, Bazball has changed the game so much forever and is saving Test cricket and is the only proper way to play the sport these days. So fair enough for Smith to assume if he got himself out, to make the score 8/393, Cummins would have no choice but to declare.

Cummins, however, is a stubborn traditionalist, who cares not one iota for the future of Test cricket and its Bazballian saviours. As far as he was concerned, the loss of Smith simply brought Nathan Lyon to the crease and the first Test also taught us that these are Australia's two best batters.

(You think I'm joking, and maybe I am a bit about Lyon. But Cummins? He's currently averaging 104 in this series.)

### THE MOUTH OF MARNUS - GRADE: F

Australia therefore batted on, reaching 416 in their first innings. It was a target that the England openers took as a challenge to run down by stumps, zero wickets down. So Zak Crawley and Ben Duckett took their guards, faced up, and set frantically off in pursuit.

> **Dan Liebke** @LiebCricket · 17h
> If I were an umpire, I'd lie all the time to batters taking guard. "Yeah, that's middle and off for sure." #Ashes
> ♡ 5   ↻ 5   ♥ 101   ılı 6,796   ↥

Seemingly the only way the England openers were going to be stopped was by the inane chatter of Marnus Labuschagne, under the lid in close, yammering on and on and on, 'liking it' in a way that nobody in earshot (which, thanks to a stump microphone turned up insanely high, included everybody watching the match) could relate to.

Was it possible to get Marnus a discussion substitute?

No, alas. His mouth had not suffered an external injury. At least, not yet.

Given the grimness of the situation, Crawley decided the only way out was to get out, which he out-and-out accomplished by running out of his crease at Lyon. Carey completed a fine stumping, yes, but it was a hollow dismissal, against a mentally defeated opponent.

> **Dan Liebke** @LiebCricket · 15h
> Good stumping from Carey, yes, but what's he like at carrying protesters off the ground? #Ashes
> ◯   ↺ 4   ♡ 61   ᴧ 2,533   ⬆

❋

## MORPHEUS OFF THE SHORT RUN

Here's what I slept through in the rest of the day's play:

> *England had their foot to the floor*
> *Racing to a big first innings score*
> *Then an injury to Lyon*
> *Got* England *brains fryin'*
> *Bounced out, the Test even once more*

# DAY THREE

## UNRULY INFANTS - GRADE: D

The third day resumed with England in a strong position, despite losing some careless wickets the evening before. With Nathan Lyon arriving at the ground on crutches as a result of his calf injury*, England simply had to wait out the bouncer barrage, tire the Australian quicks and feast on their exhaustion to surge to a first innings (and probable match-winning) lead.

(* Technically, of course, with Nathan Lyon, it's not a calf injury. It's a kid injury.)

Instead, they gleefully threw their wickets away, like unruly infants in a high chair. Yes, Ben Stokes fell to a catch from Cameron Green - the kind of thing that can happen to any of us when we least expect it.

But Harry Brook celebrated his half-century by swatting a chance straight to Pat Cummins, as did Jonny Bairstow, perhaps also wanting to get a glimpse of the Australian captain's dazzling smile.

DAN LIEBKE

With just the tail remaining, Green bounced a ball into Stuart Broad's jaw for some reason, prompting speculation of a possible Mark Wood concussion substitute for the second half of the Test.

> **Dan Liebke** @LiebCricket · 16h
> Bairstow out, but carries himself well. #Ashes
> ◯ 1   ⟲ 1   ♡ 19   ᴉ͏ᴉ͏ᴉ 2,145   ↑

Instead, Broad continued on, only to be dismissed by some Travis Head filth. Australia's number one, vegan-endorsed, GOAT substitute cleaned up a pair of England's number elevens, also taking the wicket of Ollie Robinson, who cunningly avoided the ignominy of being stumped by getting a feather on his wild waft instead.

It's no wonder they call Travis Head 'the mop'. (Although that's mostly because of the moustache, to be fair.)

### SNEERING QUESTION REVERSALS - GRADE: B+

The collapse made many England commentators unhappy. Earlier in the Test, Kevin Pietersen had gone on a rant about the players being too friendly with one another. Now, Michael Vaughan was claiming that England clearly like losing. If we add into the mix some of the bizarre rants from former Australia cricketers about Robinson after the first Test, I think we're at a key turning point in ex-player/fan relations.

Perhaps now, we, the lowly majority, can turn the classic sneering question 'How many Tests did *you* play?' back on the ex-players, safe in the knowledge that any number greater than zero is correctly seen as a devastating dent in their punditry reputation.

### FOURTH BOOKS - GRADE: B-

In *So Long, And Thanks For All The Fish*, Douglas Adams' fourth instalment to his *Hitchhiker's Guide To The Galaxy* trilogy, we are introduced to Rob McKenna, oblivious rain god, who, no matter where he travels, is followed by inclement weather. The reason for this is simple: The clouds want "to be near him, to love him, to cherish him and to water him".

It's very possible that Usman Khawaja and David Warner are also rain demigods, at the very least. For as soon as the pair padded up and prepared for Australia's second innings, Lord's clouds re-emerged, joyously hanging around the duo, providing the usual assistance to Stuart Broad and Jimmy Anderson.

And yet, somehow, Khawaja (and to a lesser extent, Warner) resisted, putting on a solid 63 for the first wicket in gloomy conditions. In fact, so skilful was Khawaja that he turned the conditions to his advantage, pulling his lone chance directly to Anderson, who was too slow picking up the dimly lit catching opportunity, the ball bursting through him for a boundary.

Jimmy Anderson, reminding everyone that his eyes are also forty years old.

# DAY FOUR

## GRIPPING CRICKET - GRADE: D-

The fourth day of the Test developed into a battle of wills between England's interminable onslaught of bouncers and Australia's interminable ducking and avoiding of bouncers.

It was gripping stuff. Assuming, that is, you enjoy being gripped by an overwhelming sense of deja vu, as ball after ball (after ball) followed the exact same path.

On the plus side, imagine how dull it would have been if England *weren't* so devoted to saving Test cricket.

Nevertheless, despite the mindless repetition of it all, England's tactics eventually bore wickets (quite literally). Usman Khawaja got bored with batting sensibly and holed out. Steve Smith got bored with playing tennis shots that saw him fall on his bottom where he could practise the shot once more and holed out.

The clever thing, from an England perspective, was how none of the catches went to Jonny Bairstow, who continued to provide a fumbling exhibition behind the stumps. Couldn't England bowl a protestor to Bairstow or something? Get his confidence back?

No. There wasn't time. Too many bouncers to get through.

Eventually, Nathan Lyon restored insanity to the contest, by hobbling to the crease to hang around with Mitchell Starc for the final wicket. Unable to take singles - to widespread booing from the knowledgeable Lord's crowd - the pair swatted a few boundaries to set England 371 to win.

❋

## MORPHEUS OFF THE SHORT RUN

Here's what I slept through in the rest of the day's play:

> *The fourth day of this peculiar Test match*
> *Ended with a controversial Mitchell Starc 'catch'*
> *Before that they lost four*
> *For a sub-fifty score*
> *Asking Stokes to once more a miracle hatch?*

# DAY FIVE

## THE SPIRIT OF CRICKET - GRADE: F

Entering the final day, England needed a further 258 runs to win, with six wickets in hand. Australia's plan was an obvious extrapolation of the previous ones in this Test. They would bounce England out.

> **Dan Liebke** @LiebCricket · Jul 2
> England commentators springing into voice today about heights of short balls. Great to hear. Something they must have thought long and hard about overnight. #Ashes
> ♡ 2   ⟲ 3   ♡ 53   ᴵᴵᴵ 3,434   ↑

Sometimes, as with Ben Duckett, this meant taking a catch down the leg side where Alex Carey had carefully (and cleverly) positioned himself. Sometimes, as with Jonny Bairstow, this meant completing a stumping after the batter dozily wandered out of their ground after ducking the bouncer.

Both dismissals were, of course, ordinary, everyday wickets that would in no way inflame heated, irrational emotion.

Ha ha ha! No. We're dealing with English crowds here, and, hence, the extra element of the Spirit of Cricket, the magnificent trump card from the inventors of the sport that allows them to take great moral outrage at seemingly random applications of the Laws of the game. Sure, sometimes they're willing to go along strictly by the letter of the Laws, as per Mitchell Starc's attempt at a catch the previous evening, which was correctly ruled not out, mostly on a technicality he could easily have avoided had he been more alert. But, other times, when cricketers are not alert to the situation, the letter of the Laws are to be ignored and replaced with a mysterious vibe about whether or not the batter should be out. I'll give you one guess as to when the vibes apply and when they don't.

> Dan Liebke @LiebCricket · Jul 2
> Carey's Ashes

Yes, that's right. The Spirit of Cricket is most often summoned into action in scenarios where England fans would quite like England cricketers to be allowed to bat on even when they're out.

The legacy of WG Grace, I guess.

## ASHES MIRACLES - GRADE: C+

Bairstow's stumping therefore caused immense and immediate fury among the Lord's crowd. 'Same old Aussies!' they chanted. 'Always appealing for wickets that the umpires give out'. Even the Lord's members, screaming drunken abuse at the Australians as they returned to the dressing room at lunch, were revealed to be appalling human beings. Difficult to imagine, I know.

Nevertheless, the fury of the crowd (and the imminent arrival of improbable number eight Stuart Broad) sent Stokes into a batting frenzy, as he threatened to repeat the miracle of Headingley, exploding into action with a magnificent 155. Broad proved to be the perfect partner for Stokes, keeping him (and the crowd) fired up with a whole heap of pantomime nonsense I'm certain not even he believed. Hero.

Here's the thing about miracles, though. If you keep doing them, it devalues the entire concept of miracles, reducing them to humdrum run-of-the-mill outcomes. A moral victory to Australia if Stokes completed the chase. Having a Pope in your side is no excuse for flaunting miracles.

And so it proved, with Carey disgustingly holding onto a skied shot that Stokes didn't even intend to hit there. Ugly stuff from the Aussies. Is this how you want to make your name, Alex? I'm surprised a keeper with so much talent resorts to hanging onto catches as well as completing stumpings. You don't see Bairstow stooping to such appalling depths.

### FADING COMIC OPTIONS - GRADE: D

Even with Stokes gone, was there the prospect for something even funnier to happen? Could, perhaps, Broad and Ollie Robinson team up to guide England home in a partnership that would have melted Australian brains the world over?

Alas, no.

Instead, Robinson was swiftly (and you're not going to believe this) bounced out.

The dream was dead. But let us not be sad for its too-soon demise but instead rejoice in ever having been gifted a glimpse of it.

And *still* there was an option for a hilarious conclusion as Mitchell Starc sconed Jimmy Anderson with (again, you're never going to believe me when I tell you this) a short ball.

The sconing, by the way, wasn't the funny bit. The funny bit was the prospect of perhaps Anderson being concussion subbed out and Chris Woakes subbed in to guide England home.

Again, alas, this comic option faded away even as it was breathed into existence. Instead, Starc knocked over Josh Tongue's leg stump and we were done. I'm never surviving three more Tests of this.

> **Dan Liebke** @LiebCricket · Jul 3
> Anyway, all a bit of fun and a good time was had by all. I'm off to bed.
> ◯ 1   ⟲ 1   ♡ 11   ıl 2,870   ⬆

Mostly, however, I'm annoyed that Bairstow's dismissal will give the England journalists an excuse to talk endlessly about that between now and the next Test, instead of viciously turning on Bazball, as nature intended.

# THIRD TEST

## HEADINGLEY, LEEDS

### THINGS BEING DIFFERENT - GRADE: A

Most of the gap between the second and third Test was spent with fans from all around the world finding example after example of England players (and coaches) taking wickets in similarly clever ways to Alex Carey's dismissal of Jonny Bairstow. You know, the one that caused such a hypocritical ruckus from those same England players and coaches. (In case you've forgotten, the same one that a typically measured Stuart Broad declared to be 'literally, the worst thing I've ever seen in cricket'. A brutal claim, which was clearly being way too harsh on Bairstow. Yes, be disappointed in your team mate's carelessness, but keep it within the dressing room.)

Not that this deterred England's finest journalistic heroes. Piers Morgan, in particular, was magnificent in his blind patriotic defence of his team, bravely swatting away each and every comparable instance, with urgent, strained cries of 'it's different, it's different', his throat raw from repeating the mantra.

Having said that, he and his similarly valiant counterparts were (and I'm sad to say this) right. The examples *were* different. But that's mostly because every single thing in the universe is different from every other thing, if only on the basis that they occupy a different position in time and space. You're never going to find a precise one-to-one mapping of two moments on one another.

> **Dan Liebke** @LiebCricket · Jul 5
> At least with mankads, I believe the England players when they say they'd never do it. (I think they're crazy, but whatever.)
>
> This, however. This is just getting sad...

But the ones that *were* uncovered each highlighted, to at least some degree, the sanctimonious English nonsense that amused everybody else so much. It must surely have been infuriating as a sane England fan to have Australia on the back foot over the Starc 'catch' nonsense, with Glenn McGrath going off, England in full control of the moral contest, only to see it thrown carelessly away in such a rash period of foolhardy hypocrisy.

## NAMING YOUR SIDE EARLY - GRADE: C (BUT OPEN TO LATER ADJUSTMENT)

England named their team for the third Test the day before the match, as has become their tradition. I can only hope that they're doing this as part of a long con, in which at some point during this Ashes series, they name an eleven a day early and then give a completely different side to Pat Cummins at the toss. That's the kind of Bazball antics I can get behind.

Into England's side came Mark Wood, Moeen Ali and Chris Woakes. Out went Ollie Pope, Jimmy Anderson and Josh Tongue.

A relief, one might have thought, to have Tongue out, given all the sniggering Travis Head wordplay from the previous Test. And then you realise that swapping Tongue for Wood won't help that situation. Not at all.

Pat Cummins, meanwhile, was too busy to name his team a day early. He was instead occupied humouring the English press, by coldly standing by his decision to play by the Laws of the game, despite their repetitive demands that he not do so. (Not that Cummins would have cared one iota about the England journos. The man faced down Steve Waugh's entire team when they all lost their shit over Justin Langer. Everything else is trivial in comparison.)

BAD BRANDING - GRADE: D-

Australia did end up making three changes to their side as well. Nathan Lyon, Josh Hazlewood and Cameron Green all out. Todd Murphy, Scott Boland and Mitchell Marsh all in.

Not that those made an iota of difference early on. Instead, it was the Mark Wood substitution that made the early difference, the fast bowler cranking up the speed. As per usual, he was often too fast for his own legs, regularly hurling himself off his feet as he delivered the ball.

His spell was a terrifying blur of pace that culminated in him blasting one through the defences of Usman Khawaja and knocking his stumps everywhere. On one hand, thrilling how Mark Wood didn't just mark the wood, he smashed it to absolute pieces.

> **Dan Liebke** @LiebCricket · 13h
> Surprised to learn that, in fact, Bazball is waiting for your keeper to get himself out in a dopey fashion, convince yourself you've been hard done by and then play like possessed furies from that point on. #Ashes
> 
> ○ 2      ⟲ 3      ♡ 20      ıl 2,624      ⬆

On the other hand, bad branding from him.

Somehow, despite his blazing magnificence, he went to lunch with just that one wicket, however. Now *that's* a proper reason to boo the Australians.

DAN LIEBKE

## SUPPORTIVE UMPIRING - GRADE: B-

Bairstow, meanwhile, continued to maintain his record as one of Australia's best performers this Ashes series. Not only did he miss a very funny opportunity to throw the ball at the stumps after the first delivery (yes, David Warner hit that ball to the boundary, but that shouldn't have stopped him), he also missed pretty much every other opportunity that came his way, in yet another display of glovenly sloppiness.

Even the umpires began to feel bad for him, signalling one of the dropped catches as a bye instead. A wonderful show of support.

This wasn't the only example of great supportive umpiring, though. Specialist Headingley comedy umpire Joel Wilson later decided from the third umpire's box that an attempt to save a four from Ben Stokes in which he was clearly touching the boundary at the same time as the ball was in his hand, should nevertheless be signalled a two.

A great gesture from Wilson, giving Stokes an opportunity to stand up for his principles and prove his devotion to the spirit of the game. Alas, Stokes fell short, shamefully accepting the umpire's decision rather than withdrawing his claim he'd saved the four.

Boos, of course, immediately rained down from the knowledgeable Headingley crowd for Stokes' poor sportsmanship. Sadly, he'll just have to live forever with not signalling to the umpires that one was a boundary. It's certainly not how the Australians would like to save a couple of runs. And so forth.

## SKETCHY RECORDS - GRADE: B

Despite all this, England went to lunch well on top, with Australia 4/91. The situation was so grim for the visitors that after the break, Mark Taylor popped up to remind Australian viewers that even though their side was dismissed here for a mere 179 back in the 2019

Ashes, they then responded by bowling out England for 67. So all hope was not lost.

(Impossible to be sure what happened after that. Records are sketchy.)

And Tubby more or less had a point, for Mitch Marsh came out and blitzed a magnificent run a ball century in the middle session. Some of his shots were so brutally struck that the camera operators started just flinging their cameras in random directions as he played his shot.

One can only assume that it's against the spirit of cricket for camera operators to follow the ball or something?

※

## MORPHEUS OFF THE SHORT RUN

Here's what I slept through in the rest of the day's play:

> *Another blistering spell from Mark Wood*
> *Worth staying up for, if only you could*
> *Fast bowling aggression*
> *In that final session,*
> *With Cummins also proving too good*

# DAY ONE

## THINGS BEING DIFFERENT - GRADE: A

Most of the gap between the second and third Test was spent with fans from all around the world finding example after example of England players (and coaches) taking wickets in similarly clever ways to Alex Carey's dismissal of Jonny Bairstow. You know, the one that caused such a hypocritical ruckus from those same England players and coaches. (In case you've forgotten, the same one that a typically measured Stuart Broad declared to be 'literally, the worst thing I've ever seen in cricket'. A brutal claim, which was clearly being way too harsh on Bairstow. Yes, be disappointed in your team mate's carelessness, but keep it within the dressing room.)

Not that this deterred England's finest journalistic heroes. Piers Morgan, in particular, was magnificent in his blind patriotic defence of his team, bravely swatting away each and every comparable instance, with urgent, strained cries of 'it's different, it's different', his throat raw from repeating the mantra.

Having said that, he and his similarly valiant counterparts were (and I'm sad to say this) right. The examples *were* different. But that's mostly because every single thing in the universe is different from every other thing, if only on the basis that they occupy a different position in time and space. You're never going to find a precise one-to-one mapping of two moments on one another.

> **Dan Liebke** @LiebCricket · Jul 5
> At least with mankads, I believe the England players when they say they'd never do it. (I think they're crazy, but whatever.)
>
> This, however. This is just getting sad...

But the ones that *were* uncovered each highlighted, to at least some degree, the sanctimonious English nonsense that amused everybody else so much. It must surely have been infuriating as a sane England fan to have Australia on the back foot over the Starc 'catch' nonsense, with Glenn McGrath going off, England in full control of the moral contest, only to see it thrown carelessly away in such a rash period of foolhardy hypocrisy.

## NAMING YOUR SIDE EARLY - GRADE: C (BUT OPEN TO LATER ADJUSTMENT)

England named their team for the third Test the day before the match, as has become their tradition. I can only hope that they're doing this as part of a long con, in which at some point during this Ashes series, they name an eleven a day early and then give a completely different side to Pat Cummins at the toss. That's the kind of Bazball antics I can get behind.

Into England's side came Mark Wood, Moeen Ali and Chris Woakes. Out went Ollie Pope, Jimmy Anderson and Josh Tongue.

A relief, one might have thought, to have Tongue out, given all the sniggering Travis Head wordplay from the previous Test. And then you realise that swapping Tongue for Wood won't help that situation. Not at all.

Pat Cummins, meanwhile, was too busy to name his team a day early. He was instead occupied humouring the English press, by coldly standing by his decision to play by the Laws of the game, despite their repetitive demands that he not do so. (Not that Cummins would have cared one iota about the England journos. The man faced down Steve Waugh's entire team when they all lost their shit over Justin Langer. Everything else is trivial in comparison.)

BAD BRANDING - GRADE: D-

Australia did end up making three changes to their side as well. Nathan Lyon, Josh Hazlewood and Cameron Green all out. Todd Murphy, Scott Boland and Mitchell Marsh all in.

Not that those made an iota of difference early on. Instead, it was the Mark Wood substitution that made the early difference, with the fast bowler cranking up the speed. As per usual, he was often too fast for his own legs, regularly hurling himself off his feet as he delivered the ball.

His spell was a terrifying blur of pace that culminated in him blasting one through the defences of Usman Khawaja and knocking his stumps everywhere. On one hand, thrilling how Mark Wood didn't just *mark* the wood, he smashed it to absolute pieces.

On the other hand, bad branding from him.

> **Dan Liebke** @LiebCricket · 13h
> Surprised to learn that, in fact, Bazball is waiting for your keeper to get himself out in a dopey fashion, convince yourself you've been hard done by and then play like possessed furies from that point on. #Ashes
> ♡ 2   ⟲ 3   ♥ 20   ıl 2,624   ⇪

Somehow, despite his blazing magnificence, he went to lunch with just that one wicket. Now *that's* a proper reason to boo the Australians.

## SUPPORTIVE UMPIRING - GRADE: B-

Bairstow, meanwhile, continued to maintain his record as one of Australia's best performers this Ashes series. Not only did he miss a very funny opportunity to throw the ball at the stumps after the first delivery (yes, David Warner hit that ball to the boundary, but that shouldn't have stopped him), he also missed pretty much every other opportunity that came his way, in yet another display of glovenly sloppiness.

Even the umpires began to feel bad for him, signalling one of the dropped catches as a bye instead. A wonderful show of support.

This wasn't the only example of great supportive umpiring, though. Specialist Headingley comedy umpire Joel Wilson later decided from the third umpire's box that an attempt to save a four from Ben Stokes in which he was clearly touching the boundary at the same time as the ball was in his hand, should nevertheless be signalled a two.

A great gesture from Wilson, giving Stokes an opportunity to stand up for his principles and prove his devotion to the spirit of the game. Alas, Stokes fell short, shamefully accepting the umpire's decision rather than withdrawing his claim he'd saved the four.

Boos, of course, immediately rained down from the knowledgeable Headingley crowd for Stokes' poor sportsmanship. Sadly, he'll just have to live forever with not signalling to the umpires that one was a boundary. It's certainly not how the Australians would like to save a couple of runs. And so forth.

## SKETCHY RECORDS - GRADE: B

Despite all this, England went to lunch well on top, with Australia 4/91. The situation was so grim for the visitors that after the break, Mark Taylor popped up to remind Australian viewers that even though their side was dismissed here for a mere 179 back in the 2019

Ashes, they then responded by bowling out England for 67. So all hope was not lost.

(Impossible to be sure what happened after that. Records are sketchy.)

And Tubby more or less had a point, for Mitch Marsh came out and blitzed a magnificent run a ball century in the middle session. Some of his shots were so brutally struck that the camera operators started just flinging their cameras in random directions as he played his shot.

One can only assume that it's against the spirit of cricket for camera operators to follow the ball or something?

※

MORPHEUS OFF THE SHORT RUN

Here's what I slept through in the rest of the day's play:

> *Another blistering spell from Mark Wood*
> *Worth staying up for, if only you could*
> *Fast bowling aggression*
> *In that final session,*
> *With Cummins also proving too good*

# DAY TWO

## THE PEOPLE'S PRINCE - GRADE: B-

Pat Cummins dismissed Joe Root from the second ball of the day to turn the Test emphatically back Australia's way. When Jonny Bairstow also fell shortly after to Mitchell Starc, Australia were like a starving seafood lover at an all-the-lobster-you-can-eat restaurant, greedily eyeing off the tail.

It was the perfect time to bring on The People's Prince, Todd Murphy, in his Ashes debut. Allow him to settle into the series now that he'd made the step up from Nathan Lyon's understudy to Australia's front line spinner.

For his first five overs, he did a fine job, going for just five runs. That's the great thing about Todd Murphy. He's a spinner who will skilfully hold up one end with smart bowling *and* later file your tax returns.

(Explanation of joke: because he wears glasses that make him look a bit like an accountant.)

## THE MEN'S ASHES

### PAIN THRESHOLD DEBATE - GRADE: C

Of course, Murphy's next 14 balls went for 31 runs, before he finally terminated Ben Stokes' wild thrashing from his fifteenth. Stokes' knock was inspired by an eight-ball, 24 run blitz from Mark Wood who, impossibly, scores runs faster than he bowls. Ironic, really, given that his surname should so easily encourage the adjective 'lumbering'.

Kickstarted (not literally) by Wood, Stokes teed off. He didn't just hammer Murphy either. All the Australian bowlers suffered from Stokes' aggression. But was this secretly a clever ploy from Pat Cummins' men? It's by now well-known that Stokes' decision to take on the England captaincy was accompanied by the monkey's paw curse of simultaneously turning into an eighty year old man. And it looked for all the world like any one of those sixes might be the one that finally shattered Stokes' ailing back into a thousand crumbling pieces of vertebrae.

But if it was a ploy from Australia, it was one based on a faulty premise. Because the fact is that Ben Stokes lies all the time about being injured.

Yes, the commentators go on and on about his high pain threshold. And yet... what if it's the exact reverse? What if Stokes secretly has an incredibly *low* pain threshold? After all, he seems to be in constant agony about things that are so objectively minor that they don't hinder his ability to play unbelievable cricket in any way.

> **Dan Liebke** @LiebCricket · 11h
> Going to bed in this series is fraught with peril. All manner of crazy stuff tends to happen during sleeping hours. #Ashes
> ◯ 1   ⟲ 1   ♡ 40   ᴵᴵᴵ 5,208   ⤴

If so, it's a savvy ploy from the England skipper. And even *more* savvy of him to not let on by stepping up to bowl in Ollie Robinson's bowling crease absence. Well played, Ben Stokes. Well played, indeed.

❄

DAN LIEBKE

## MORPHEUS OFF THE SHORT RUN

Here's what I slept through in the rest of the day's play:

> *Australia looking to stretch their lead*
> *Setting a target, what do they need?*
> *Their best batters staying in?*
> *Rather than losing wickets to spin?*
> *At least, I guess, they survived Mark Wood's speed*

# DAY THREE

## ALEX CAREY'S HAIRCUT - GRADE: A

With rain about on the third day, all talk turned, naturally enough, to Alex Carey's hairdresser. More precisely, to claims from Sir Alastair Cook that the Australian wicketkeeper had got a haircut, then refused to pay the barber who'd provided it.

Will Carey's reign of insidious terror in the mother country never end? It doesn't even matter that the hairdresser thing turned out to be utterly false and swiftly discredited. The fact that it's plausible to an actual English knight is enough to condemn him, in my opinion.

Do we need to start a GoFundMe for Carey's UK haircuts? Because I'll do it. Alternatively, perhaps Carey will prove his innocence by growing his hair as long as possible in the remaining weeks of this tour, to the point where he is given the nickname 'Hairy Carey'. (Ideally, in this scenario, he would also grow quite contrary and/or start hanging around Donaldson's Dairy.)

Either way, Carey's haircut is already making a mockery of Stuart Broad's claim about what he'll be remembered for.

## SNEAKY POUNCING - GRADE: D

With the rain seemingly settled in, pretty much all of Australia headed to bed. That's when England pounced, sneaking in a final period of play while we were all asleep (including, seemingly, several members of the Australian team).

Luckily, Travis Head was still awake and, despite wickets tumbling around him, he teamed up with the tail to add 54 for the last two wickets, setting England 251 for victory as he thrashed sixes and boundaries over the heads and in between scattered fielders, before cleverly manipulating the strike at the end of each over to safeguard his numbers ten and eleven.

Not so fun now, is it Ben?

# DAY FOUR

### EXPLODING HEADS - GRADE: B+

Chasing 224 on the final day with ten wickets in hand, the match oscillated back and forth, with Mitchell Starc, in particular, heroically striking again and again every time England threatened to pull away.

England, for their part, innovated, sending in Moeen Ali at three (Mo*three*n Ali?) after Starc trapped Ben Duckett. (Trapped him LBW, to be clear. He didn't snare him in a mousetrap or anything.)

But Starc was having none of it, castling Moeen with one that blasted through his defences and knocked middle stump out of the ground.

> **Dan Liebke** @LiebCricket · Jul 9
> Fucken hell, Mitch #Ashes
> ◯ 3   ⟲ 1   ♡ 24   ᶦᶫᶦ 3,579   ⬆

Australia were inching their way in front of the match, and threatened to pull ahead still further when Cameron Green briefly substituted in the gully while, I dunno, Mitch Marsh went and had a poo or something.

The prospect of Green taking a screamer and Piers Morgan's head exploding was thrilling. But, alas, too much to hope for, even in this most gripping of series.

## TESTING BLOWS - GRADE: C+

When Pat Cummins inevitably accounted for Joe Root, it brought Ben Stokes to the crease, with 120 still needed. Given that England were already within range of victory via one of Stokes' miracle innings, the honourable thing for Cummins to have done at that point would be to immediately concede the Test.

Instead, the shameless Australians continued to play the Test to its conclusion.

The key blow for the visitors seemed to be the nut shot that felled Stokes (followed almost immediately by his dismissal). Yet despite the blow to his nether regions, Stokes somehow managed to crawl desperately back to his crease.

A shame, really. What a test of the Australians it would have been to see if they'd run out a man whose testicles had just been shattered. Is it really the way you want to win a Test?

No, of course not. And so Australia didn't, losing by three wickets as Woakes and Wood scrambled home for England. Another great Test sees us heading to Old Trafford with Australia 2-1 up and everything still to play for.

(Well, not *everything*. Just the Ashes, really.)

# FOURTH TEST

## OLD TRAFFORD, MANCHESTER

# DAY ONE

## WEATHER-RELATED WEIRDNESS - GRADE: A-

With heavy rain forecast for the fourth and fifth days of the Test, and Australia needing only a draw to retain the Ashes, every single lover of cricket - and particularly Bazball-style cricket - let out an enraged scream when Pat Cummins once again called the toss wrong.

For it meant that Ben Stokes could opt to bowl first and try to work their way as quickly as possible through the twenty wickets they would need to win the Test. Maddening. Because we all know that if England had been asked to bat first, they would have almost certainly declared at lunch on, I dunno, 7/180 or something.

Instead, the only real weather-related weirdness we got came in the form of too much sunshine during the first session, as glare reflecting off a metal beam of some kind distracted the batters.

The obvious solution was to take a mid-over drinks break and put Stuart Broad on the case. As we saw all the way back in Adelaide a decade ago when Broad came out to face peak Mitchell Johnson, there is nobody better equipped to wreak the maximum amount of comedy out of some kind of sight screen issue than Broad.

And so it proved with the humour veteran skilfully rearranging members of the crowd in such a way that they would cover the reflection. Magnificent.

> **Dan Liebke** @LiebCricket · Jul 19
> A wicket straight after (the scheduled time but not actual time of) a drinks break. #Ashes

## BOO ELIMINATION - GRADE: C

Australia looked to bat England out of the match with their lengthened batting line-up. (Quite literally lengthened, of course, with the return of Cameron Green to the side, who, you may have heard, is rather tall.)

But despite pretty much everybody getting a start, the home side kept fighting back to take wickets and prevent Australia from putting the match out of reach.

On the plus side, at one point, the ball deflected off Steve Smith's bat as he was completing a run and he held up a hand to signal to Marnus Labuschagne that they would be taking no overthrows.

A lovely gesture from Smith, and a timely one. After all, following the Jonny Bairstow stumping a couple of Tests ago, we were reliably informed that a display of the Spirit of Cricket would mean that English crowds would be won over by the Australians' grand sportsmanship. All past misdemeanours would be forgiven and never again, would an Australian cricketer be booed in England.

Or, as it turned out, this *wouldn't* be the case, with, by my count, Steve Smith (on dismissal), Alex Carey and Pat Cummins (on arrival at the crease) all being heartily jeered.

In retrospect, Smith should have taken the overthrows.

## UNDEAD SWAMP ELVES - GRADE: D

It was hard to keep track of how deep we were into the Australian batting line-up at any moment. Yes, wickets were falling. And yet more and more batters kept coming, as the scorecard climbed towards 300.

But, eventually, around about the time Mitch Marsh strode to the crease at number six, England had made their way deep into the Australian all-rounders. When Cameron Green joined him, and Mark Wood came back on to bowl, the scoreboard was suddenly confronted with 'Green Wood Marsh', which sounded like some horrific haunted elven swampland.

However, the prospect of undead swamp elves was blown away by a burst from Chris Woakes, leaving us with easily the most normal day of the series so far, as Australia finished on 8/299.

Hopefully something much more mad (eg batters colliding mid pitch, a juggled boundary catch thrown over the rope, Ben Stokes deputising a small child or robot to field at leg slip, etc) will happen tomorrow.

# DAYS TWO AND THREE

### THE PARTY STAND - GRADE: F

For the second and third days of this Test, we were seated in the 'Party Stand'. It was unclear exactly what kind of party we were dealing with, but based on many of the comments heard throughout the day, it was the kind of party you definitely hope never gains power.

For example, most of the second day was spent listening to a grown man shouting 'CHEAT!' at random intervals and with little discernible provocation. Did this become amusing after the 400th or 500th bellow? Alas, it did not. But kudos to this gentleman for giving it a red-hot go.

Could he have taken joy out of watching Zak Crawley and Joe Root put on a blistering double century partnership that swiftly overhauled the Australians' total in the middle session and more or less ensured England could not lose this Test? Sure, perhaps *some* cricket fans might get enjoyment from watching their team do so thrillingly well. But does that really compare to the exquisite experience of being able to scream incessantly at Josh Hazlewood that he's 'a fucking prick'? Of course not. Cricket fandom comes in many forms and we should appreciate all of them.

More delightfully, the third day saw this drunken conversation on the Tour de France emerge.

"Cycling isn't a sport."

"It is."

"No, it's fitness."

"But they're trying to get to a point faster than somebody else."

"It's fitness."

"It's literally a race."

"Okay. It's a sport. But it's one I'm not interested in."

Which was an amusing back and forth. Was it sorely lacking in speculation about how much of a cheating prick, say, Mitch Marsh was? Yes. But, again, that's okay.

## NOT DECLARING - GRADE: C

The blitzkrieg of the England batters continued well into the third day. Australia's initial plan had seemed to be to force Ben Stokes to declare two wickets down on day two, and then have every England fan turn on him when it all went terribly wrong. It was a plan that had seemed to be going swimmingly (well, the first half anyway), but Stokes' decision to bat on soon put paid to that.

Instead, it appeared that England planned to only bat once, and hope that the purported washouts of days four and five were highly exaggerated. Pretty good work from Australia, I think, to take away England's well-known preference for batting last in the Test.

What was poorer play from Australia was their insistence on every now and then foolishly taking wickets that would bring them closer to having to bat again. For with every England batter who came to the crease locked in for at least a half-century, Stokes couldn't resist allowing them their milestones.

At lunch, the difference between the two sides' totals in the first innings was precisely Zak Crawley's score of 189. A fitting marker for a declaration, even if, on most occasions, a difference of a Crawley knock is hardly definitive.

Yet, Stokes still batted on. Rain forecast be damned. He was not declaring, the innings ending instead in perfectly comical fashion when Jonny Bairstow was left stranded on 99* after James Anderson was trapped LBW.

> **Dan Liebke** @LiebCricket · 18h
> Stokes deliberately not declaring as a riposte to those who dared criticise his decision to do so in the first Test. #Ashes
> ♡ 1    ⟲ 1    ♡ 24    ıl 2,289    ⬆

Still, if Stokes loses the Ashes because he was having too much fun watching his lads have a thrash to remember to declare in time to win the Test, that may be the most Bazball thing in existence.

### TAG TEAMING - GRADE: C+

And so Australia needed to bat out a session and a half to get to the predestined rain. Could they do it?

Well, Dave Warner tried, but only reached 28 before inside edging a delivery from Chris Woakes onto his stumps. Unlucky for Warner who probably thought (after watching Crawley at close quarters just the day before) that inside edges were the key to a flurry of boundaries.

Usman Khawaja, Steve Smith and Travis Head, meanwhile, were all blasted out by Mark Wood's pace, before Mitchell Marsh (a man who on close inspection this Test seems to have a body that's too big for him. Or maybe too small. It's hard to tell. Either way, it doesn't fit properly) and Marnus Labuschagne saw Australia to stumps four wickets down and still 162 runs away from the unlikely prospect of forcing England to bat again.

Job done. Over to you, Manchester weather.

# DAY FOUR

## MANCHESTER WEATHER - GRADE: C

The Manchester weather lived up to its billing for much of the fourth day, digging in its bid to secure Australia the Ashes, before a lapse in (cloud) concentration gave England an opportunity.

For suddenly, the middle session was dry enough to play. England could wrap up the remaining wickets, level the series and send us to the fifth Test for a decider.

Or, alternatively, Marnus Labuschagne and Mitch Marsh could bat mostly untroubled for a couple of hours, diminishing the deficit between the two teams and rarely looking like losing their wicket. To be fair, under gloomy conditions, they were assisted by the umpires, who decreed that Mark Wood was too fast to be allowed to bowl. But to be even more fair, I've been saying this for *ages*.

The conditions were so dim that umpire Nitin Menon didn't see Labuschagne edge a wide delivery off Joe Root straight through to Jonny Bairstow shortly after bringing up his century. DRS swiftly rectified that, but it couldn't rectify the return of the rain at the tea break that ended the day's play.

> **Dan Liebke** @LiebCricket · 16h
> Completely unclear to me why Bairstow was up to the stumps with Marsh on strike. Surely he didn't intend to stump a batter who was habitually out of his crease. #Ashes
>
> ◯ 4   ⇄ 2   ♡ 72   ɪʟɪ 5,038   ⇪

> **Dan Liebke** @LiebCricket · 16h
> (Or, y'know, attempt to do so.)
>
> ◯ 1   ⇄   ♡ 11   ɪʟɪ 1,474   ⇪

Yes, it'll be a disappointing result if the rain comes and saves England from a now likely defeat, but there's not much you can do about the weather.

> **Dan Liebke** @LiebCricket · 15h
> If I've calculated correctly there have been precisely thirty overs today which means a fifty percent refund of ticket price. Do not come back out for one more ball, you bastards. #Ashes
>
> ◯ 1   ⇄ 2   ♡ 29   ɪʟɪ 4,846   ⇪

# DAY FIVE

## MORE MANCHESTER WEATHER - GRADE: A

As it turned out, the rain *did* arrive in time to save England on the fifth and final day of the Test, with no play possible as the Old Trafford surface instead slowly but surely turned into a namesake tribute to the two batters who would otherwise have resumed their innings.

Rather absurdly, we had been forced to buy premium tickets for the fifth day because all general admission seats were sold out. It did, however, give us a very comfortable location called The Pegasus Lounge, with a great vantage point from which to watch covers and outfields grow increasingly damp. If you're going to be at a soaked ground, I can highly recommend this as the way to do it. *Especially* considering we got our money refunded at the end of the day after no play.

And so this was how we farewelled Manchester. With the Ashes retained, the ground sodden and our ticket price refunded. Sure, Old Trafford hadn't provided a Test in terms of sheer quality to match the one we saw at Headingley last time around. But it did provide one that made a lot of England fans cross. And that has its own merits. In the spirit of the week, we'll call it a draw.

## MORAL VICTORIES - GRADE: A

It was deeply unsatisfying, of course, for Australia to retain the Ashes based solely on this rain-sodden draw. (Oh, and also winning the first two Tests.) Or, at least, that's what England fans and/or journalists began swiftly assuring us. On the other hand, I am reminded of the excellent website, whohastheashes.com?

Still, Old Trafford had given England an absolutely thumping moral victory. Add in the two moral victories in the first (Ollie Robinson felt like they'd won) and second (Jonnie Bairstow was stumped when he would rather have been allowed to keep batting) Tests and this series has been a total moral thrashing. Concerning for Cummins and his team.

Hopefully, they can scrap together a consolation moral victory at the Oval.

From an England perspective, they've spent this series learning about the existence of such things as rain, opponents protecting the boundary, and stumpings. Can't wait to see what shock element of the sport awaits *their* startled eyes in the final Test.

# FIFTH TEST

THE OVAL, LONDON

# DAY ONE

## FIFTH TEST CHANGES - GRADE: B

For the fifth and final Test of the series, Australia made just the one change to their team, with Todd Murphy replacing Cameron Green. A good change, not only because it added an actual spinner to the attack, but also because Green could just theoretically spend the entire time on the ground fielding at gully anyway, as whichever bowler had most recently finished their spell took a short break in the dressing room. Good tactics.

The reshaped bowling attack required yet another variant on Australia's palindromic bowling attack, which now read:

- Starc?! Rats!
- Oh, so Josho!
- Too fast! A Pat's afoot
- Todd, dot!
- No! Si. No! Si. Bison is on.

The other change to the team? Pat Cummins' call of 'tails' finally proving successful, as Ben Stokes lost his first toss for the entire series.

Although, of course, England will claim that it *felt* like he won it.

DROPPED CATCHES - GRADE: C-

Cummins asked England to bat first, and after an unconvincing opening new ball foray from Mitchell Starc and Josh Hazlewood, he came on to bowl a magnificent spell that threatened with every single delivery, yet somehow resulted in only the one wicket, that of Zak Crawley. (In yet another sign of how mad this series has become, the dismissal was rightfully described in commentary as 'The big wicket of Zak Crawley'.)

One of the reasons that Cummins took only the one wicket was that Australia's cordon decided that, since England batters only got one hit in the previous Test, they'd give them each a couple of bats this innings. Lovely bunch of lads, the Australian fielders.

Further helping their reputation, Australia *didn't* field Green at gully, despite having a perfect right to do so. If they had done, Harry Brook would almost certainly have been out twice to ones that flashed through gaps between third slip and gully. (Or thrice if you assume Green would have also caught the rebound off Alex Carey's drop.)

Now, when it comes to matches, you're not going to believe what, according to conventional cricket wisdom, catches do to them. And yet, despite dropping five chances and missing a run out, Australia still knocked England over for a seemingly subpar 283. (But, yes, yes. A 283 total scored fast! Always important to note that, apparently.)

## MORPHEUS OFF THE SHORT RUN

Here's what I slept through in the rest of the day's play:

> *Heading to bed, openers batting under lights*
> *Tough scenario, one designed for true sleepless nights*
> *Yet Khawaja got through*
> *(Although not Warner, that's true)*
> *So come day two, Australia can aim for much greater heights*

# DAY TWO

## TURGID BATTING - GRADE: C

Australia began the day on 1/61, the kind of score that upon waking up and checking it, had you assuming some of the last session must have been rained out.

But no, the Australian batters were simply determined to stubbornly score at half England's rate. Just for the hell of it, seemingly. And they continued that plan into the second day, meandering along, seeing themselves safely past the follow-on mark of 83 in the 41st over of their innings.

Oh sure, they copped a lot of criticism for only scoring 54 runs in the entire session, with many pundits claiming that it was too slow, too dull and too obviously emphasising the 'turd' in 'turgid batting'.

On the other hand, from an Australian perspective, it was better than a session in which they scored twenty more runs but also lost four more wickets.

Because that's precisely what happened in the second session, as England's attack tore through Australia's middle order. Heck, even

Jimmy Anderson took a wicket, and he's a very old man. The worm had, if not turned, then at the very least, flicked the indicator to let the worms behind it know that it was about to do so.

## FUNNY UMPIRING DECISIONS - GRADE: A-

When Alex Carey fell, slapping a delivery from Joe Root straight to Ben Stokes, Australia were 6/170, still more than a hundred behind England's total. Mitchell Starc was out shortly after, on 7/185, and Pat Cummins joined Steve Smith at the crease, the prospect of winning the series (rather than merely drawing it and retaining the Ashes) in grave peril.

So, of course, Steve Smith almost immediately ran himself out, charging through for a second run on the arm of a mystery substitute fielder.

Despite looking for all the world as if he was gone, the third umpire assessed the situation, spotted that Jonny Bairstow had dislodged (maybe?) a bail before gathering the ball, and ruled that, since it was so funny for Bairstow to once again muck up a wicket-taking opportunity, Smith was not out.

Good umpiring to not just take the Laws of the game into consideration but also the comedy of the moment.

Not that it mattered. Stokes would almost certainly have withdrawn the appeal, anyway. Substitute fielders running out the opposition's best batter? Fine for a gutter fight such as 2005. You wouldn't want to take a wicket that way these days, though. Great sportsmanship from Ben.

Still, awful behaviour from both teams. I was going to go to bed at tea, FFS. Instead, with all this nonsense taking place (and subsequent antics such as Todd Murphy going full Mark Wood with the bat on Mark Wood with the ball), I was tricked into staying up until the end of the day's play.

# DAY THREE

## THREE QUESTIONS - GRADE: B

England began the third day of the Test with a looming number three problem, with Moeen Ali unable to bat in the position due to his time off the field with a groin injury.

Who would fulfil the role instead? It was the greatest three question since *Monty Python and the Holy Grail*. Various players were spotted with pads on, raising the prospect that perhaps when the first wicket fell, it would simply be a foot race to the middle to decide who batted in the role.

Or perhaps it would be Moeen himself. After all, after two hours, he would be able to bat wherever he pleased. With England setting off in helter-skelter Bazball fashion, erasing the first innings deficit in the first over and barely slowing up from there, there was a very real prospect that the openers would bat out the entire first session and render the question moot.

But then Alex Carey heard a faint nick off the edge of Ben Duckett's bat that nobody else could detect and, more importantly, convinced

# THE MEN'S ASHES

Pat Cummins he wasn't imagining things. Carey hears as if he has Adam Gilchrist's ears. Great wicketkeeping lineage.

As it turned out, Duckett's wicket saw Ben Stokes emerge at first drop for England. Huh. Who knew the Kneeless One was so sharp in a foot race?

## PERFORMATIVE BITS - GRADE: D+

At no point did England let up, however, motoring along at around five runs an over for most of the innings as they looked to set a big fourth innings chase for the Australians.

> **Dan Liebke** @LiebCricket · 15h
> Guys, I don't want to freak you out but I'm hearing reports that England have scored more quickly than Australia this #Ashes series.
> ◯ 6   ⟲ 3   ♡ 119   ᴵᴵᴵ 5,449   ⬆

The rapidity of the scoring soon had the (English) commentators cackling with delight.

"The wins at Edgbaston and Lord's seem a long time ago now."

"So long ago they shouldn't count?"

"Yes."

(Some of this dialogue may have been implicit.)

Sure, the odd wicket fell, but the runs continued. Jonny Bairstow arrived in the middle and continued doing the thing he now does where he performatively returns to the crease, waiting for the ball to be dead, as if this wasn't exactly what he should have been doing all along.

"Oh, is this what you expect me to do?? Put my bat behind the crease while the ball is alive?! Well, okay, here it is. Happy now?"

DAN LIEBKE

It's amazing he had time to score 78 (103) with all the effort he was putting into this bit. Shows how well he was batting, I guess.

## STUART BROAD'S RETIREMENT - GRADE: F

As England continued their way to 9/389 at stumps, the cameras cut to Zak Crawley on the balcony, doing a crossword but also looking up the answers to the crossword as he did so. A very Bazball approach to the classic word puzzle. Changing the way crosswords are solved.

"We're fostering a dressing room environment where no crossword question is 'too hard'," Crawley later explained. "We're challenging the orthodoxy of solving the clues yourself. When Baz first came in, he said to us 'the answers are right there, in the back' and we checked and they were. Such a great feeling to know that. Just takes the pressure off."

Speaking of crosswords, however, you don't want to hear what I muttered when I woke up the next morning to the news that Stuart Broad had retired. Crosser words have never been spoken.

I'd go so far as to say Broad's retirement has ruined this entire Ashes series. You might even say the glorious genius has rendered it void.

What a bloody hero.

❄

## MORPHEUS OFF THE SHORT RUN

Here's what I slept through in the rest of the day's play:

> *Stuart Broad has fucken retired,*
> *Stuart Broad has fucken retired,*
> *He's retired,*
> *He's retired,*
> *Stuart Broad has fucken retired.*

# DAY FOUR

### REWRITING NARRATIVES - GRADE: C

The penultimate day of this Ashes series began in normal fashion. A guard of honour for the retiring Stuart Broad (who, by the way, revealed that he was retiring because he's at his happiest in the dressing room right now with a team full of mates and he wants to leave on that high. Big mistake from Stokes to create such an environment, in my opinion), followed by the great man turning down singles, hitting a six from the final delivery he faced in Test cricket (a bouncer, obviously) and then wandering off after James Anderson was trapped LBW at the other end.

It meant Australia needed 384 runs to win. Impossible, obviously, and yet, a few hours later, as the rain came tumbling down, with David Warner and Usman Khawaja both having reached half-centuries and Australia 0/135, the feeling was that England were the team happier to get off the ground.

Because in the intervening innings, England had shown few signs of a breakthrough. Moeen Ali was too injured to bowl effectively. Mark Wood was not turned to, for some reason, perhaps also injured. Stuart

Broad was unthreatening. Chris Woakes similarly. And Jimmy Anderson had become the most prolific 41-year-old bowler of beamers I've ever seen (overall tally: 1).

> **Dan Liebke** @LiebCricket · 12h
> Can't believe the rain's going to save England AGAIN! #Ashes
> 💬 21    🔁 36    ♡ 619    📊 40.6K    ↑

It left Australia needing just 249 further runs for a stunning narrative-rewriting victory on the final day. Still rather a lot, really. You'd probably continue to back England to take the ten required wickets.

Nevertheless, to have every single pundit question everything they held as self-evidently true as little as twenty-four hours ago as a result of a record run chase that recast Australia as 3-1 series victors would be hilarious. (Not that they'll get there, of course, but it'd be very funny if they did. (But they won't. (Funny if they did, though. (They won't.))))

# DAY FIVE

CHANGING BALLS - GRADE: B

And so we came to the mad final day. One that began with Australian fans and commentators complaining furiously about the replacement ball the umpires had chosen for England. Unlike the previous ball, this one swung more and saw the rapid demise of not just Usman Khawaja and David Warner but also Marnus Labuschagne, triggering a truly phenomenal amount of moaning about the situation from Australian fans and commentators.

> **Dan Liebke** @LiebCricket · 17h
> Australia fighting back strongly in the moral #Ashes thanks to a ball change. Didn't expect them to show such fortitude but great to see.
> ♡ 3    ↻ 6    ♡ 111    ᴵᴵᴵ 4,766    ⚓

Warner must have felt particularly hard done by, dealing as he did with the unlucky triple blow of rain interrupting his innings, a newish ball replacement and Jonny Bairstow holding onto a catch.

The ball, of course, wasn't the only thing that changed. The unfair umpires also swapped out the tired and clueless England attack from the prior day for a threatening and focused set of bowlers. None more so than Chris Woakes who was challenging the batters with every delivery.

Nevertheless, Travis Head's arrival at the crease saw Australia steady once more, to the point where England asked the umpires if they could get a different Travis Head to the crease. Maybe one without a moustache?

### GOING FULL HERSCHELLE - GRADE: A-

When the request to change Travis Head was denied, Ben Stokes decided he'd entertain everybody with a spontaneous recreation of Herschelle Gibbs' famous dropped catch, leaping to pluck an edge from the bat of Steve Smith, only to then spaffle the ball out of his own hand while going to toss it up.

It was a strange piece of play made even stranger when the rest of his team talked him into reviewing the chance.

A magnificent piece of nonsense with which to head into lunch. Had Ben Stokes dropped the Ashes? No. The Ashes were already safely in Australia's hands. But he certainly seemed to have dropped England's chances to deny Australia an outright win of the series to go with their Ashes retention.

Not quite as pithy a sledge, though.

### LOSING LITERAL AND METAPHORICAL HEADS - GRADE: D

But instead of Australia resuming after lunch and knocking off the final runs for victory, we instead had a couple of hours of rain. England shamefully changing the non-rain weather for weather that was obviously far rainier, trying to send us all to bed.

When play resumed, we were told it was for a mental 52 over final session. And then, in yet another enraging moment for Australian fans, the umpires cruelly changed the 52 over final session for one that was instead clearly only 47 overs.

Maddening stuff. Even more maddening when it became much shorter than those scheduled 47 overs, thanks to an Australian collapse. Australia lost their literal Head, then their metaphorical ones, as Woakes and Moeen Ali tore through the middle order.

Finally, with Todd Murphy and Alex Carey offering brave, futile resistance, it was over to the great man, Stuart Broad. The mad genius left us all in the style we've come to expect, reprising his bail-swapping gag from the first innings to dismiss Murphy, before almost certainly contemplating a farewell mankad of Josh Hazlewood, only to instead take Carey's outside edge to give England a 49 run win that levelled the series 2-2.

A fine result. But, nevertheless, looking back on it, I think we can all agree that this Ashes series will primarily be remembered as the 2-0 GOATwash. Certainly, that's how I'm choosing to remember it.

# THE WOMEN'S ASHES

9 FEB 2023 - 13 MAR 2023

# TEST MATCH

## TRENT BRIDGE, NOTTINGHAM

# DAY ONE

## TEST SNITCH CRICKET - GRADE: B

The Women's Ashes, which has been a multi-format series for quite a while now, began this time with the Test match, still shamefully worth a mere four points in the overall scheme compared to three ODIs and three T20s, each worth two points.

The Test match should be a golden snitch in this multi-format Ashes. Worth at least a thousand points. No, a million! A billion!

Sure, some will say it's out of whack to have one match in the series be worth so much more than the rest that it renders the others essentially invalid. Okay, fine. Then to make it fairer, why not have, say, four more Tests, all worth the same amount as the first one. (Under this scheme, you don't even have to play the white ball games at all. Unless you want to, as maybe a separate lower-valued series.)

It's a crazy idea for an Ashes series, but it's one that just might work.

## CAPTAINCY UPS AND DOWNS - GRADE: C

As it is, given the current state of the women's game, we instead celebrated a milestone for Ellyse Perry who, in her sixteenth year of international cricket, has now played half as many Tests as Cameron Green.

To celebrate, she moved up to number three in the Australian batting order, filling the spot left vacant by Meg Lanning. England, for their part, announced their eleven a day before the Test began. A big mistake, in my opinion, for them to reduce from the squad of fifteen. Play the four extra players. Give yourselves a chance.

But England captain Heather Knight overcame that initial error magnificently at the toss, claiming after Alyssa Healy elected to bat that she was always going to bowl anyway. Correct captaincy from Knight. Always claim you were intending to do what you're forced to do. Give them nothing.

## A LACK OF SWAY - GRADE: D

Australia's debutant Phoebe Litchfield looked imperious in her Test debut, racing her way to 23 via some glorious strokeplay until she foolishly left a delivery from Kate Cross that crashed back into her pad.

Even more foolishly, she convinced herself that she was out, not reviewing the decision despite the ball-tracking later showing that it would have missed the off stump.

Yes, I've long maintained that not playing a shot should trigger the inclusion of a virtual fourth stump in the ball-tracking algorithm. But, and here's the key, Phoebe, this idea has not yet been implemented. And almost certainly never will be. I don't have any sway whatsoever over international cricket. Review the decision.

## WAYWARD TODDLERS - GRADE: B

You know who does review decisions? Ellyse Perry, that's who. For when Knight threw the ball to *her* young debutant, Lauren Filer, with the England speedster zipping one past Perry's defences, trapping her on the pad first ball, the umpire raising an erroneous finger, Perry was having none of it

She sent it upstairs immediately, where the third umpire approved the inside edge and overturned the decision. Always great to see a wicket from the first ball of an Ashes debutant overturned by DRS. Now I wish Gatting had reviewed Warne's first Ashes delivery.

Still, it would save a lot of DRS time if the third umpire simply looked at the scoreboard. "Perry out for 10? Self-evidently ridiculous. You'll have to change your on field decision."

Nevertheless, this Lauren Filer person felt like she would be a problem going forward. She was fast. She moved the ball through the air and off the seam. She had a mystery ball (sure, it was a mystery ball that involved her dropping the ball in her run-up and then chasing after it as it rolled down the pitch past the umpire like it was a wayward toddler. But that still counts!)

❄

## MORPHEUS OFF THE SHORT RUN

Here's what I slept through in the rest of the day's play:

> *Australia were batting just fine*
> *Against an attack that felt quite benign*
> *Then bother and fuck.*
> *Healy gone for a duck*
> *And Perry caught out, ninety-nine*

# DAY TWO

## DUN-DUN SOUNDS - GRADE: D

England returned for the second day, as is their right, no doubt hopeful that with Australia seven wickets down, they could wrap up the innings quickly.

Their plan? To use the excess Laurens in their attack to work their way through the Australian tail. And, to an extent, it worked, with Lauren Bell jagging one back in from outside off stump to bowl Alana King.

Is it fair for England to have such a Lauren-heavy attack? Obviously not. Choose one of Lauren Filer or Lauren Bell. You can't have both. Frankly, the ICC needs to clamp down on this. Enforce some Lauren order.

(Dun-dun sound!)

England's other plan (apart from bowling Sophie Ecclestone for thousands of overs) was to get their fingers on every ball struck back at them and deflect it onto the stumps.

This obviously takes tremendous skill and was the clear result of countless hours of net training. Having said that, it was also incredibly surprising, especially considering their previous stance on the matter, to see them go for so many attempts at run outs at the non-striker's end.

## BEING ELLYSE PERRY - GRADE: B

None of the assorted tactics worked on Annabel Sutherland, however, who continued serenely along, unbothered by anything England threw at her (most often cricket balls, to be fair (also, bowled usually, rather than thrown)).

The biggest threat to Sutherland seemed to be her own desire to be the new Ellyse Perry. Given such a lofty goal, would she follow her senior all-rounder's lead and be dismissed for 99?

No, as it turned out. Instead, she made her way to the century. A decision that had many of us disappointed. Doesn't want the Perry mantle. Not willing to aim that high.

But it turns out we were absolute fools. Sutherland *does* want the Perry mantle, and instead was taking the long view as Australia were bowled out for 473.

Sutherland finished on 137*, which means she now has a Test batting average of 77.50, quite literally the closest number she could get to Ellyse Perry's 77.36.

(Well, she *could* have gone on and been dismissed for 214, which would have given her a batting average of 77.33, just 0.03 off Perry. But, and this is crucial, 0.03 *behind* Perry. Instead, she's 0.14 ahead of that hopeless has-been. A statement.)

❄

DAN LIEBKE

## MORPHEUS OFF THE SHORT RUN

Here's what I slept through in the rest of the day's play:

> *473, England were asked to pursue*
> *A target too high, surely, to outdo*
> *But Beau(mont) is (not) afraid*
> *Her century making the grade*
> *As England finished on 218 for 2*

# DAY THREE

## FOOT-CENTRIC WICKET-CLAIMING CONVICTIONS - GRADE: C

Not content with scoring a century on the second day of the Test, Tammy Beaumont decided she'd score *another* one on the third day, moving her score from 100* overnight to 208, when she was the last batter dismissed in England's innings.

No matter what the Australians tried, they seemed unable to budge her. They tried catching her by way of a rebound off her boot, but then forgot to appeal loud enough to convince the umpires to send the decision upstairs (or to have enough conviction in their foot-centric wicket claims to send it up themselves).

They also tried trapping her LBW via leg-spinner Alana King, only for Beaumont to have enough conviction in *her* foot-centric wicket claims to send the decision upstairs, where it was overturned when the ball was found to have pitched a bee's dick outside leg stump. (A fact confirmed by a passing apiarist called in to remove a beehive that was found on the Trent Bridge nets. (The bit about the net beehive is not a joke.))

## SUBATOMIC PARTICLES - GRADE: C-

What the Australians didn't seem to try until it was much too late was that thing they usually do where they crush the opposition side into subatomic particles. A pretty silly misstep, to be frank. Why would you move away from a tactic that's worked so well in previous series?

Instead, England, led by Beaumont's record-breaking innings, inched closer and closer to improbable parity with Australia. At one point, they even looked certain to cruise past it and establish a first innings lead. (If you can imagine such a thing.)

Luckily, however, the Australians decided they'd go back to giving the molecular obliteration thing a try. And, hey, it worked! Tahlia McGrath suddenly tore through the England tail, in the process finally uncovering a weakness in Tammy Beaumont's game.

Namely, getting her to bat with a number eleven who she clearly did not trust one iota and have her thrash wildly at an Ash Gardner delivery only to be bowled.

One to put away in the memory banks for sure.

❄

## MORPHEUS OFF THE SHORT RUN

Here's what I slept through in the rest of the day's play:

>  *A match that hadn't gone entirely as planned*
>  *Still saw the Aussies resume, ten runs in hand*
>  *So, hey, that's a freebie*
>  *For Beth and young Phoebe*
>  *To amass an unbeaten 82-run opening stand*

# DAY FOUR

## SLOPPY WORDPLAY - GRADE: D

The fourth day of the Test began with England employing a stunning new tactic of giving every Australian batter a life via a dropped catch. A bold ploy from the home side, even if it was one that didn't seem to have an immediately obvious link to cricketing success.

And yet, somehow it did? Phoebe Litchfield was the first to benefit from a dropped chance, raising prospects for some wordplay in the vein of Phoebe *Mis*field. On reflection, however, the wordplay didn't quite work. It implied she was the one who misfielded, instead of being the one who benefited from it. Also, a dropped catch is much worse than a typical misfield.

And also once more, by the time we'd really thought through the ramifications of the sloppy punwork, Litchfield was already out, leaving yet another delivery that struck her on the pad. Fortunately for her, this time around the ball continued on after hitting the pad, removing the bails as well. No need for anguish about whether or not to review.

Everything's coming up Litchfield.

### DORKY WIZARDS - GRADE: A-

Emboldened by the Litchfield wicket, England proceeded to also give Beth Mooney and Ellyse Perry lives, offering the pair dropped chances of varying difficulty.

Perry proceeded to punish the England fielders, with some exquisitely placed strokes through the covers. To be frank, I admire *anybody* who possesses sufficient batting skill to be able to actually place a cricket shot. I'm mostly just grateful if I actually connect with the ball. Imagine also having a say in where it goes after that glorious moment of triumph.

Despite this, Perry was soon out to the marauding Lauren Filer, a tall, dorky, fast bowling wizard, who is so much fun that, even when she's taking Australian wickets, I can't stay angry with her.

Maybe there was something in this dropping tactic from England? Was it making the Australians overconfident? Perhaps.

Although they didn't even bother with it for Tahlia McGrath, the impatient Filer blasting through her defences before anybody had even been given the opportunity to spill a chance off her.

Bad play from Filer. Hopefully, captain Heather Knight had a word for her as the players headed off to lunch.

## MORPHEUS OFF THE SHORT RUN

Here's what I slept through in the rest of the day's play:

> *An early bedtime at lunch,*
> *Meant I missed wickets, in fact a whole bunch!*
> *Ecclestone took five*
> *To keep England alive*
> *Before Gardner struck a huge counter-punch*

# DAY FIVE

## ASHLEIGHT GARDNER - GRADE: A

The fifth day began with England trying to once again regenerate, a la the top tier X-Men franchise mainstays such as Wolverine, Deadpool or Rocky Balboa, after yet another cellular disintegration blow from Australia in the previous evening session.

This time, they were unable to do so, finally succumbing to the spin bowling of Ashleigh Gardner, who proceeded to take eight wickets in Australia's second innings. Ashl*eight* Gardner, if you will.

The haul of 8/66 and 12/165 for the match - the best in Australian women's Test cricket history - gave Australia victory by 89 runs and a 4-0 lead in the multi-format series.

Imagine having players scoring a double century or taking ten wickets in a Test and still not being player of the match. *And* having that not even be a controversial decision. That's the precarious situation in which England find themselves.

Of course, it's a massive advantage for Australia to have a woman named Ash in the women's Ashes. An unfair advantage? Yes, undoubtedly.

# T20S

# FIRST T20

## EDGBASTON, BIRMINGHAM

### MORPHEUS OFF THE SHORT RUN

Awful times for the Women's Ashes T20s. 3:30am? Why would you play cricket then? Crazy. Here's what I slept through in the first match:

> *A 154 run chase, game on!*
> *An Aussie win sees Ashes virtually won*
> *But a silly time-slot,*
> *Meant my rhymes got*
> *More desperate than a penultimate ball run*

# SECOND T20

## KENNINGTON OVAL, LONDON

### MORPHEUS OFF THE SHORT RUN

The second T20? Also at a silly time. Here's what I slept through in the second match:

> *Winning a match, time to try it*
> *So England sent out Danni Wyatt*
> *She got them off to a flyer,*
> *And made Australia require*
> *187, and they fell short? I don't buy it.*

# THIRD T20

## LORD'S, LONDON

MONKEY'S PAW WICKETS - GRADE: D

Hey, look at that! I was awake for one of the women's T20s. Good for me.

Australia were asked to bat first and agreed to do so on the condition that they could score 150 from their twenty overs. After some heated haggling back and forth between the captains, it was finally agreed that Australia would be permitted to reach 155 on the condition that top scorer Ellyse Perry would be dismissed in a classic monkey's paw good news/bad news scenario.

That scenario?

**Bad news:** Ellyse Perry is out LBW

**Good news:** She's reviewing the decision

**Bad news:** The first replay shows she's *very* plumb in front

**Good news:** This can't be confirmed because DRS is down

**Bad news:** This means the umpires stay with the original decision

**Good news:** But Australia don't lose their review

**Bad news:** They only had 11 balls left anyway

### UNEXAMINED TECHNICAL PROBLEMS - GRADE: D+

England unleashed their criminal weather yet again during the innings break, with the target adjusted to 119 runs from fourteen overs.

Not that it mattered much. Danni Wyatt and Alice Capsey raced their way to the total and, despite a panicky hiccup (easily the worst kind of hiccup) with just a handful of runs remaining, England stumbled over the line, winning the T20 leg of the multi-format series 2-1 and keeping the women's Ashes alive.

> Dan Liebke @LiebCricket · 3h
> IDEA: Get Wyatt out #idea
> ♡ 4   ⟲ 1   ♡ 7   ᴨ 3,382
>
> Dan Liebke @LiebCricket · 3h
> Replying to @LiebCricket
> IDEA: Get Capsey out #idea
> ♡ 1   ⟲   ♡ 2   ᴨ 1,066

This is annoying, because I don't even know *how* to update the www.whohasthewomensashes.com website. Frankly, it's not a technical problem I've ever thought to examine.

So, come on, Alyssa and co. Let's sort this out in the ODIs, huh?

# ODIS

# FIRST ODI

## COUNTY GROUND, BRISTOL

### APATHIE À COURT TERME

Women's ODIs are at a better time than the T20s, especially since I've made my way to Paris in time for them. Alas, however, French disdain for the sport is palpable and unforgiving. Here's what I missed in the first match:

> *I couldn't make my TV set work,*
> *Nor my virtual private network*
> *But as technology crashes,*
> *England level the Ashes*
> *Does this annoy me a lot? You* bet, *jerk!*

# SECOND ODI

## AGEAS BOWL, SOUTHAMPTON

### DEFENCE ENTRUSTMENT - GRADE: A-

With scores level in the multi-format series, and the prospect of rain washing out the final ODI, the fate of the women's Ashes potentially rested on this one match.

That's why it was good from an Australian perspective to have Ellyse Perry out there, anchoring virtually the entire Australian innings, making a calm, measured, albeit occasionally overly-reliant-on-English-drops 91 from 124 balls.

Perry's innings helped Australia reach 7/282 after being sent it. (Also a big help? Georgia Wareham going absolutely silly in the final over and smacking 26 runs.)

At the innings break, sensible Australian pundits were calling on Alyssa Healy to give Perry the new ball as well. Entrust the entire defence of the Ashes to this woman. You know it makes sense.

## BAD DECISIONS - GRADE: C

But did Healy listen? No, she did not. To be fair, by what mechanism would she have done so? She's a busy woman with only a limited innings break that's far too short with modern technology to consolidate the opinions of all the pundits into an easily digestible consensus for her to take in before beginning the fielding innings.

Nevertheless, opener Tammy Beaumont got England off to a rollicking start, raising the obvious question: Haven't we seen enough of Tammy Beaumont this Ashes series? The obvious and correct answer: yes.

On the plus side for Australian fans, Beaumont did confess to having leg-byed a ball that was originally called a wide, costing England both a run and an extra delivery in their innings. Almost certainly nothing that would have an impact on the match.

Less rollicking was Sophia Dunkley, who pottered around, struggling for timing. A shame, then, for Wareham to dismiss her three balls into her spell. Could the Australans recover from this setback?

## SPIN QUADRUPLETS - GRADE: A

Well, yes, as it turned out. Australia went full 'I'm seeing double' with not just 'spin twins' but 'spin quadruplets', all of whom had a significant impact on the chase. Player of the match Alana King took the three key wickets of Beaumont, Heather Knight and Alice Capsey. Ash Gardner continued her reign as the coolest person I know (or the coolest person I *would* know, if I knew her, which I don't) by also taking three wickets and a catch. And Wareham and Jess Jonassen bowled tightly in the final overs, securing a three run win, even as Nat Sciver-Brunt threatened to steal victory with a defiant, unbeaten century.

It was Sciver-Brunt's third century in ODIs against Australia, all in losing causes. Should Australia always allow her to score tons? It's a seemingly crazy tactic but also an effective one? Worth exploring perhaps now that the Ashes have been safely retained.

Still, this series is what the 2005 men's Ashes should have been. A plucky England side fighting valiantly against a champion Australian side but (and this is the important point) not winning the series. Much more satisfying because we can then heartily praise the opposition but still keep the Ashes (to confirm: www.whohasthewomensashes.com). Proper cricket.

Nevertheless, a great performance from this England team to push Australia all the way. (See? The system works.)

# THIRD ODI

## THE COOPER ASSOCIATES COUNTY GROUND, TAUNTON

### ICARUS OFF THE SHORT RUN

Ashes safely retained in the previous match meant my inability to watch this one due to travel to, from and between airports was less stressful, as this limerick makes clear:

> A long and hard-fought Ashes tour,
> Brought relief, once the urn was secure,
> It meant a trip on a plane
> (And a break due to rain)
> Were trivial setbacks to endure

# SOUTH AFRICA V AUSTRALIA MEN'S ODI SERIES

7 SEP 2023 - 27 SEP 2023

# FIRST ODI

## MANGAUNG OVAL, BLOEMFONTEIN

### MODERN AUSTRALIAN CAPTAINCY - GRADE: B+

During the preceding clean sweep in the T20 series, Mitch Marsh had shown his promise as a leader, scoring unbeaten half-centuries batting at number three, prompting questions about a cricketing world in which Marsh could never be dismissed while captaining Australia. Fortunately, this crisis was averted in the third T20 when he was out for 15, giving him the batting average as captain of 186. Suck on that, Bradman.

Even more promising, however, was his response on winning the toss in this, the first ODI between the two sides. Marsh decided Australia would bowl first so they don't have to field in the cold of the Bloemfontein evening. This is *precisely* the kind of forward-looking climate thinking we expect from modern Australian skippers. Welcome to the fold, Mitchell.

## CREASE ANTAGONISM - GRADE: B-

Just as in the T20s, Marcus Stoinis was given the new ball. And swung up a storm with it, further cementing his status as my new favourite opening bowler. Not for the wickets he inexplicably takes, but for the ways in which he inexplicably takes them.

As Mark Nicholas pointed out on commentary, Stoinis's improvement with the ball could be attributed to him attacking the crease more. So much so that at one point he body-slammed it in his follow-through. This dedication to crease antagonism must be applauded.

His willingness to get right up in the face of the crease was rewarded when he somehow bounced Quinton de Kock out for 11 (31), caught in the deep by Cameron Green. Earlier, de Kock had announced that he would retire from the fifty over game after the upcoming World Cup, but this turgid innings suggested he may have jumped the gun, retirement-wise.

## REJECTING CAMERON GREEN'S HANDS - GRADE: D-

The de Kock innings was emblematic of a sluggish effort from South Africa, who kept losing wickets at a steady rate while simultaneously struggling to accelerate the scoring on a tricksy pitch.

There were chaotic run outs, balls that kept low, and nibbles outside off stump. Aiden Markram scored a breezy 19 (14), before top-edging a delivery from Green. Wicketkeeper Alex Carey called for the catch and comfortably took it. A surprising decision, really. Yes, Carey has the gloves, but Cameron Green has Cameron Green's hands.

Through it all stood captain Temba Bavuma, who convinced Marco Jansen not to throw his wicket away for a while. But after Jansen went, along with the rest of the tail, including Kagiso Rabada, who couldn't resist following and feathering a spinning delivery from Adam Zampa (timely newspaper headline: Rabada Unable To Leave

Turning Man), Bavuma decided enough was, as is so often the case, enough.

With just number eleven Lungi Ngidi left, Bavuma began thrashing away, farming the strike and, in the process, brought up both his century and South Africa's 200, as the home side eventually reached 222, with the skipper carrying his bat. Okay, Bavuma.

The highlight of this late innings counterpunch? Carey once again hogging a skied ball that Green would almost certainly have pouched, and dropping the South African skipper on 88.

And the England fans will try to tell you Carey is unsporting.

※

## MORPHEUS OFF THE SHORT RUN

Here's what I missed in the second innings, in limerick form:

> *After some top order thrashing and flaying*
> *Australia collapsed in a manner dismaying,*
> *But Marnus subbed in,*
> *To secure a cool win,*
> *A fine effort from a man not even playing*

# SECOND ODI

## MANGAUNG OVAL, BLOEMFONTEIN

### GUILLOTINE BATTING - GRADE: C

For the second ODI, Australia were asked to bat first. "Good gracious, Temba," replied Mitch Marsh. "I am overwhelmed by your boundless generosity and unparalleled sportsmanship in bestowing upon us the esteemed opportunity to bat first in this One Day International! My heart swells with gratitude as I humbly accept your incredibly considerate offer. All of Australia thanks you for this extraordinary honour."

He may have been taking the piss.

> **Dan Liebke** @LiebCricket · 12h
> There are too many moustaches in this ODI. Please eliminate four.
> #SAvAUS
> ♡ 14    ılıl 1,511

Also taking the piss? Travis Head opening the batting, whose onslaught at the top of the order saw Australia blast their way to a century within the first batting power play of ten overs. With South Africa feeding him endless short balls outside the off stump, there were more Head cuts than the French Revolution.

## LOOMING PENALTY RUNS - GRADE: B+

The introduction of Tabraiz Shamsi to the attack put a momentary halt on Australia's batting frolic, as the left arm wrist spinner dismissed Head and Marsh in consecutive deliveries, the latter to an ill-considered first ball reverse sweep.

The golden duck meant that Marsh continued his trend of performing worse with the bat with every innings in every format in which he leads Australia. Presumably, then, the remaining ODIs will either see him lose the captaincy or have penalty runs bleed from him like a decapitated 18th century French aristocrat.

Five penalty runs from the first ball faced for deliberately short running? Bring it on, Captain Mitch.

## MATCH-ALTERING MANICURES - GRADE: D

Whatever hope South Africa had of clawing their way back into the contest after those quick wickets was soon lost, however. First, the umpires insisted their claws be filed down to a safe length by an ICC-sanctioned manicurist. More importantly, though, David Warner and Marnus Labuschagne immediately put on a 151-run partnership at around seven runs per over. The contest devolved further into an elongated T20esque boundary-blasting exhibition, to which I responded as I pretty much do to every such T20 match.

Which is to say, I fell asleep.

To be fair, a few glasses of wine may also have contributed to my slumberous reaction. Either way, I missed both Warner and Labuschagne bringing up their inevitable, wildly-celebrated, existentially unsatisfying tons as Australia finished on, let's say, 8/392. (Sensible batting from Australia not to surpass 400 - they've never won an ODI against South Africa when amassing a tally beyond that benchmark.)

DAN LIEBKE

An impressive effort from Labuschagne, in particular, proving he can contribute as a middle order batter in the starting XI, rather than just playing to his established strengths as a world class concussion substitute.

❄

MORPHEUS OFF THE SHORT RUN

Here's what I missed in the second innings, in limerick form:

> *Bavuma and de Kock got off to a flyer,*
> *Chasing 392, could they go one run higher?*
> *No, they could not.*
> *They instead only got*
> *269, which is lower, unless you're a liar*

# THIRD ODI

## SENWES PARK, POTCHEFSTROOM

### NEVER FORGETTING - GRADE: C

South Africa batted first, sent in by megalomaniacal madman Mitch Marsh, under the fool impression that he could prevent Temba Bavuma and Quinton de Kock from adding 146 for the first wicket in 22.5 overs.

Where he got that idea, nobody knows, although the new ball spells from Josh Hazlewood and Marcus Stoinis *did* keep the openers briefly under control. Indeed, after the seventh over, the South Africa 'Manhattan' featured twin towers in the fifth and seventh overs standing proudly above the low-rise, three runs per over cityscape that surrounded them. A beautiful 9/11 tribute. #neverforget

### STRONG BRANDING FEELINGS - GRADE: D

The urban sprawl of the South African innings soon grew out of control, however. Bavuma and de Kock authorised the development of eight, ten and twelve runs per over skyscrapers, which soon littered the innings horizon. The sensible city planning of the Australian attack proved no match for the openers' haphazard development regime.

As the pair continued their indiscriminate rezoning of the partnership into an industrial boundary-producing district, the realisation dawned on the Australians that they may be chasing an enormous total. A target so large, in fact, that Marnus Labuschagne might have to bat at four *and* substitute in at eight if Australia were going to chase it down.

Sure, moustachioed demolition expert Travis Head was belatedly introduced to the attack to break the partnership, but all that succeeded in doing was bringing Aiden Markram to the crease, who finished with 102 not out as South Africa blasted their way to 6/338.

Still, 10*2**, Aiden? 101 not out was right there. Markram's ongoing refusal to embrace the massive branding potential of his palindromic name is now just sad. Self-destructive behaviour that he'll someday regret. (Apologies for coming over all Preachy Brendon McCullum there, but that's just how strongly I feel about palindromic branding.)

※

## MORPHEUS OFF THE SHORT RUN

Here's what I missed in the second innings, in limerick form:

> *Warner blasting away, the big chase was on*
> *But then he was run out and all hope was gone*
> *Not even Labuschagne*
> *Could do it again,*
> *They needed to sub in a clone of The Don*

# FOURTH ODI

## SUPERSPORT PARK, CENTURION

PREPARING FOR THE WORLD CUP - GRADE: D

ODIs as far as the eye could see (ie, while scrolling through an app containing scorecards of live matches)! With a World Cup imminent, three matches were taking place simultaneously, as everybody desperately worked on their final preparations for the tournament. South Africa v Australia. England v New Zealand. India v Bangladesh.

Could I OD on ODIs?

> **Dan Liebke** @LiebCricket · 10h
> I see the England selectors have dropped Ben Stokes. Harsh, but it's the only way he'll learn to go on with it when he gets a start. #ENGvNZ
> ◯   ⟲   ♡ 5   ıl 1,172   ⤒

No. But surely to *properly* prepare for the World Cup, these teams needed to not just be batting, bowling and fielding. A World Cup campaign is a multi-faceted thing. It's just as important to practise keeping a close watch of the others' matches, postulating, perhaps, how it would really help our semi-final prospects if New Zealand beat England. Or closely monitoring India's NRR and how it compares to your own and how *that* might affect the chances of progressing. Hoping for the very worst for those nations you least wish to face in the finals. Little skills that come to the fore in the back half of a tournament.

(Then, of course, it should rain with the match tied on DLS and South Africa knocked out based on, I dunno, a countback to the time Brian Lara single-handedly beat them.)

COMPLACENCY - GRADE: D

I don't know whether Australia were rehearsing these important observational wishing skills during the fourth ODI against South Africa. But I do know that up until I went to bed, they seemed to more or less have the bowling and fielding bits under control.

By the second drinks break, I'd watched the Australian bowlers not really take a lot of wickets, but also not really let the South African side get away.

Nathan Ellis had bowled Reeza Hendricks with the kind of delivery that puts the Ellis back in 'I'm so *jealous* of people who can bowl like that'. Josh Hazlewood had also put an end to Quinton de Kock's masochistic nominatively deterministic batting.

The commentary of Pommie Mbangwa, which always makes me feel like everything's going to be okay (honestly, let the man talk me through my day sometime), lulled me into sleepy complacency, even as his co-commentators offered little Zen koan riddles to ponder: "As always, Hazlewood is back to his best."

It was all very sedate. So I went to bed and missed Heinrich Klaasen getting very silly indeed.

## MORPHEUS OFF THE SHORT RUN

Here's what I missed, in limerick form:

> *Heinrich and Dave Miller - holy Jesus fuck!*
> *To chase 416, you'd need lots of luck*
> *Instead, Travis Head's broken hand*
> *Sent groans through the land*
> *Mitch returning the team to Pat in a big garbage truck*

# FIFTH ODI

## THE WANDERERS STADIUM, JOHANNESBURG

LUMBERJACKERY - GRADE: B+

Now, finally! The decider to a series that had gripped two nations. Admittedly, Australia were not necessarily one of those nations, given the time zone in which the series was played and the ongoing semi-finals in assorted winter football codes. And based on the local crowd being far more interested in highlights of a World Cup rugby union match shown on the big screen between overs, South Africa may not have been one of the nations gripped by the series either. But surely there are two countries somewhere that have been gripped. Get a United Nations task force onto this and sort it out.

Australia, gluttons for punishment, decided they'd chase an enormous target yet again, and struck early via a Marnus Labuschagne run out of Temba Bavuma.

Bavuma was called through for a single by Quinton de Kock after being struck in the ribs. Too polite to hold up a hand to say 'hey, Quinton, I'd really rather grimace in pain for a few moments, thanks, mate', Bavuma set off late, and Labuschagne ran him out with a direct hit.

What I particularly liked was that before the stumps were felled, Quinton de Kock shouted 'TEMBA!'. A post-cricket career in South African-accented lumberjackery awaits him.

Still, pretty cruel of the commentators to go on and on about how Bavuma was 'a long way short'.

(Explanation: because he's not a very tall man.)

## WAITING IMPATIENTLY FOR THE FIREWORKS FACTORY - GRADE: C

Because this match was a day game, it meant that I was unlikely to go to bed before the South African batters went into completely insane batting mode, smashing a zillion runs per over.

But who would it be? Not de Kock, who was caught by Cameron Green after Nathan Ellis found his edge. Silly from de Kock. Why would you edge it to any of the half-dozen slip positions that Green is covering?

Nor was it Rassie van Der Dussen. Or the previous match's hero, Heinrich Klaasen, who was bowled by Adam Zampa for just six. A lot of talk after that wicket about Zampa 'getting his revenge' on Klaasen. But given that Zampa had the equal worst ODI bowling figures ever in that prior match, surely he needed to dismiss Klaasen for the equal worst *batting* figures (that's 0 from 31 balls by West Indies batter Runako Morton, in case you're wondering) to enact proper vengeance.

Besides, Aiden Markram and David Miller were having their own fun against Zampa, launching him into the crowd on a semi-regular basis, without ever really entering the very silly mode of the previous match. (Having said that, should Zampa stop being hit for six? A tactical question for Australia to ponder heading into the World Cup.)

DAN LIEBKE

A desperate Mitch Marsh drew upon a classic palindromic plan to deal with Markram.

That plan?

*Stun Markam nuts.*

The blow to his testicles slowed Markram down just enough for Australia to dismiss him via some first-ball-in-ODIs Tim David Filth. At this stage, the prospects for a South African explosion seemed limited indeed.

Fortunately, just as all hope seemed lost, Andile Phehlukwayo came to the rescue, smashing three sixes and a four off the final over to see South Africa past three hundred yet again.

THE ASIA CUP FINAL - GRADE: A-

Any thought of watching a bit of the Asia Cup Final during the innings break was scuppered by Sri Lanka's... well, I hesitate to call it batting.

Mohammed Siraj tore through the Sri Lanka top and middle order, taking four wickets in his second over to have his opponents 5/12 and in an amount of strife that could only be described as 'dreadful'. And while Sri Lanka recovered slightly after that, they could still only muster an even fifty runs for their entire innings. An innings that ended just in time to coincide with the South Africa-Australia innings break. Rude.

As Australia were starting their reply to South Africa, India wrapped up the Asia Cup Final with just ten wickets and 263 balls to spare. Hopefully the organisers had whatever the opposite of a reserve day is ready to go.

Mostly, however, I'm impressed that Siraj took four wickets in an over and didn't take a hat trick.

Back in the match I'm ostensibly reviewing here, Australia were batting better than Sri Lanka (despite a couple of early wickets), and when I went to bed at the first drinks break, Mitch Marsh and Marnus Labuschagne seemed to have things more or less under control in the run chase.

Of course, Marsh was then out by the time I'd finished brushing my teeth.

❈

## MORPHEUS OFF THE SHORT RUN

Here's what I missed, in limerick form:

> *Captain Marsh out while I was brushing my teeth,*
> *But Marnus still there, and full of belief*
> *Except he was soon gone,*
> *And no-one else kicked on,*
> *The series finally over, so that's a relief*

# ABOUT THE AUTHOR

Dan Liebke is a comedy writer, who was a regular contributor for MAD Magazine in Australia for two decades before coming to his senses and turning his comic focus to cricket.

Dan is a genuine all-rounder, equally inept with both bat and ball, and he steadfastly believes that cricket is the funniest, and hence best, sport that humanity has ever invented.

TO DO

- Visit Dan's cricket web site: liebcricket.com
- Support Dan on Substack or Patreon for early access to a variety of benefits: newsletter.liebcricket.com or patreon.com/liebcricket
- Follow Dan on Twitter (@liebcricket), Mastodon (@liebcricket@mastodon.social), BlueSky (@liebcricket.bsky.social) or whatever other social media platforms arise. I trust you to recognise the pattern.

## ALSO BY DAN LIEBKE

**The Instant Cricket Library** - An anthology of excerpts from imaginary, unpublished and other hard-to-find cricket books

**The 50 Greatest Matches in Australian Cricket (of the last 50 years)** - Excellent cricket matches in which Australia played. Fifty of them to be precise.

**The 50 Greatest Australian Cricketers (of the last 50 years)** - Excellent cricketers who played (and/or currently play) for Australia. Fifty of them to be precise.

**50 Great Moments in Australian Cricket** - A tour of why cricket is the greatest sport, via a sometimes-tentative link to moments in Australian cricketing history. Fifty of them.

**The 10 Greatest World Cup Wins in Australian Cricket** - A top ten countdown of best cricket World Cup wins for the only nation for which such a countdown is applicable, Australia.

**Dan Liebke's Wasted Review of Cricket 2022** - This book, but for the period of October 2021 to September 2022

**Dan Liebke's Wasted Review of Cricket 2022/23** - This book, but for the period of October 2022 to February 2023

**C.R.I.C.K.E.T.** - A comedy cricket book compiling comedy cricket essays, analyses, sitcom scripts, thought experiments and other fleshed out comedy cricket premises

These books are all available for purchase at liebcricket.com/store or your local book store of choice.

**Dan Liebke's Wasted Review of Cricket in 2022**

Copyright © 2023 Dan Liebke

All rights reserved.

❀ Created with Vellum